Empowering The Next Generation

A "How To" Guide To Starting A Youth Leadership Program

Carl L. Camon, Ed.S

Included In This Edition

A Five Step Guide To Starting A Community Youth Program
101 Websites For Youth & Community Related Grants
A Sample Youth Leadership Curriculum
Youth Leadership City Life Scenario Activity Guide
State Agency Contact Guide For All Fifty States
Contact Guide For Every Municipal League In The United States

www.mayorsyouthinstitute.com

TRAFFORD PUBLISHING™

Order this book online at www.trafford.com
or email orders@trafford.com

Most Trafford titles are also available at major online book retailers.

Printed in the United States of America.

ISBN: 978-1-4269-2634-1 (sc)
ISBN: 978-1-4269-7833-3 (e)

Library of Congress Control Number: 2010901045

Trafford rev. 7/30/2011

Trafford
PUBLISHING®   www.trafford.com

North America & international
toll-free: 1 888 232 4444 (USA & Canada)
phone: 250 383 6864 ♦ fax: 812 355 4082

Dedication

I dedicate this book to my wife Angela and our four children, Carl, Aaron, Camille, and Candace, for their love and for their support of my endeavors over the past fifteen years in public office. Without the support of my mother, Madine Camon, I would have probably left public office a long time ago. Thanks mom, for your encouragement. I will always remember my greatest role model, and that was my father, Jr. Bishop L.J. Camon. He taught me well. This book is also dedicated to communities who have realized the value of training our next generation of leaders, and to the youth around the world who have accepted the challenge to become world-class leaders. I offer a special thank you to the City of Ray City, and all of its citizens for allowing me to serve them as their mayor for five terms. Much appreciation goes out to the Georgia Municipal Association (GMA) for the awesome training they have provided to me for nearly fifteen years, and to the National League of Cities for inviting me to share the successes of our youth leadership program, with cities all across our nation.

About the Author

Carl Camon is a true public servant. He was appointed by the governor to serve on the State of Georgia's County & Municipal Probation Advisory Council, where he served as both a member and as Chairman. Carl served on Georgia Municipal Association's (GMA) Board of Directors, Executive & Budget Committees, and as Chairman of GMA's Environment & Natural Resources Committee. He also served as a member of GMA's Training Board. He served as a member of the Southeast Georgia Rural Development Center Board of Directors and on the Berrien County Chamber of Commerce. He served as Vice-President of the Berrien County Democratic Party. He is a nationally known advocate for youth, and he was invited to attend the Congress of Cities Conference, by the National League of Cities (NLC) based in Washington, D.C. for four consecutive years, to serve as a City Showcase Presenter, where he shared the successes of the Mayor's Youth Leadership Institute (MYLI) of Ray City Program, with cities and organizations across the country. Just recently, Carl was once again invited to share the youth program with the National League of Cities at its Congress of Cities Conference, for the fifth time. Carl Camon founded the MYLI in the year 2000. The program focuses on effective leadership skills, local, state, and federal government issues, abstinence, drugs, alcohol, and tobacco prevention, school dropout prevention and community involvement. He was also invited to the West Wing of the White House along with other leaders from across the country to discuss issues pertaining to youth and after school initiatives. He is an honorably discharged U.S. Air Force Veteran, who served during peacetime and wartime. He has served for five terms, as the first African American Mayor of Ray City, which is located in South Georgia. Carl was instrumental in obtaining over three million dollars in grant funds for Ray City, during his tenure as mayor. He is an educator with 15 years experience, and he possesses both an earned Master's Degree in Special Education and an earned Education Specialist Degree in Educational Leadership, from Valdosta State University. He and his wife Angela, who is also an educator, are the owners of Teacher Advocacy & Protection (TAP), Inc., an organization that provides training for teachers and advocates for teachers' rights.

Contents

Step Five

Introduction

Empowering The Next Generation – *A "How To" Guide To Starting A Youth Leadership Program* is one of the many resources that you may use to assist you in starting a youth program in your own community. It is a simple and easy to read guide that walks you through the process in five easy steps. Each of the five steps consists of six mini-steps that further explain how to approach the rigorous, but rewarding task of successfully starting a youth program. You may choose to follow the guide in the sequence it is written or you may pick and choose which step you want to use first. An example of an actual curriculum, which I designed for the Mayor's Youth Leadership Institute program, is included as a part this guide, as well. In an effort to help ensure your success, contact information for various substance abuse and behavioral health agencies in all fifty states is included in this guide, as well as the addresses and phone numbers of forty-nine Municipal Leagues, and information for 101 grant providers. I am confident that your use of this guide will offer insights to help you to become better prepared to accomplish your goal of starting a youth leadership program in your community.

Empowering Our Youth

Empowerment begins at home, but the sad fact is that many of our youth don't really have a place to call home. Often times the light gets brighter and brighter as they walk toward or ride the school bus to school. For many of our youth, that same light grows dimmer and dimmer as they depart school and journey back to their respective homes. What does this tell us? It tells us that great educational environments work. So, what do we do once our youth return back to their communities? There is no possible way that we can be in the homes of every child who has a need, but we sure can invite them to community youth programs. We can educate them and empower them to take responsibility for their education and their future, so that they can triumph over generations of poverty and defeat.

I believe that our youth are empowered through education. As a classroom teacher, with fifteen years experience, I see things from a different perspective. What I am about to say about today's youth, as it relates to education may sound a bit critical, and it may be a bit opinionated. Nevertheless, it must be said, and I will venture to say that my views are not too distant from the views of educators and those in the field of education all across our country. The first step to recovery, in any situation, is to admit that a problem exists. My narrative below briefly addresses some of the issues and problems that we are faced with in today's "New World of Education" and it offers some solutions to those problems.

There is no doubt that our youth, and the process of educating our youth has drastically changed from what it used to be years ago. I am sure that there are those who remember when a community really cared about education; students went to school for the purpose of learning; teachers entered the teaching profession to teach; and principals did their jobs to make sure that all of the above was taking place. I remember the days when the entire community took an interest in raising the children of that community. Nowadays, the members of some communities are afraid to lend a helping hand or approach situations involving our youth, for fear of becoming the victim themselves. That is why it is so important for us as concerned citizens, to lead the way in reclaiming the youth of our communities. The main goal of this guide is to help you start a youth program that will make a positive impact in the lives of the youth in your community, and throughout your city as a whole.

We are all linked together in some way or another. In order to take that first step, we must find out what links are missing from the societal chain. The breakdown of the traditional family unit and the unsuccessful attempts to appropriately address critical issues, such as drug and alcohol abuse, teen pregnancy, and the near collapse of our educational system are just a few issues that helped to create the missing links in this chain. As stated earlier, I am an educator and I am going to give you my "two cents" worth, regarding my opinion of why we are experiencing this near collapse. These opinions led me to take action, on behalf of our youth. Before I could take action, I had to come to the realization that education or the lack thereof, had a significant impact on communities. Once I came to that realization, it was easy for me to boldly speak out regarding the fact that our educational system needs some major overhauling, and it needs it now. I promise you that after I am through venting about my views of the current state of education, I will offer some insights on how to start a community youth program.

Okay, here we go. In various schools, administrators are faced with threats from students and their parents, and teachers are often times placed in precarious and sometime unsettling situations within the classroom. Over testing students has also become commonplace in today's classroom, and in some cases, it causes undo stress to many students and teachers. I feel very passionate about education, as you will discover as you read the remainder of this narrative.

Some teachers and staff are literally afraid to say anything to a young boy or girl, for fear of retaliation from them, their parents, or the parent's attorney. When they do have the courage to say something, then more times than not, it is taken out of context, and the teacher spends a good portion of time trying to explain what he or she meant. What kind of message are we sending to today's youth? When there is the creation of a school law, rule, mandate, handbook, etc., for students to follow, Boards of Education, administrators, teachers, and parents must support it wholeheartedly. If not, our youth will receive a mixed message, which will lead to their own interpretations of what is to be expected. We have to remember that we are the adults, and they are the youth. That is not to say that we should not listen to what they have to say. We should make every effort to combine their ideas with ours, and make the best decision for all parties concerned.

Socialization has become the norm in some educational environments. Many of today's youth are inundated with music, and watching music videos that are saturated with violence, sex, and rebellion. Some of our youth take these videos at face value, and sadly enough, in some cases what they see is reality. If they see sagging pants, they wear sagging pants, if they see extra short skirts, they wear extra short skirts, and in my opinion the sagging pant and short skirt syndrome has made a negative impact on many of our youth. Many naysayers often respond by saying that each generation has its' own woes, and I would tend to agree. However, even though past generations have made profound statements, the vast majority of them had some respect for authority. It is sad, but it is a fact that the intent of some of today's youth is to disrespect authority.

There were times when parents respected teachers and gave them all the support that they needed to help educate their children. To some degree, that has changed, and the respect has taken a downward spiral. Most teachers are honest, and have earned the respect from many, however even the most respected teachers are targets for lawsuits and the like. There were times when an innocent handshake or hug was just that, but these days if you ask a student his or her name or touch a student in any way, it could be misconstrued as inappropriate. Cases against teachers are referred to the state agency or commission that governs the conduct of teachers. Many times even if the teacher is found not guilty, the stigma remains and the lives of some teachers are ruined forever. Strong and swift reprimands and punishment should be applied if a teacher or administrator violates the teacher's code of ethics, and the trust that parents and society place in them. However, that same strong and swift action should be applied to help bring frivolous cases to justice.

The availability of qualified teachers all across our nation has dwindled in years past. Strategic and drastic measures have been taken to recruit more teachers, but efforts often fall short. There are educational movements like "No Child Left Behind", and assessments like the Criterion Reference Competency Test "CRCT", various High School Graduation Tests, and "AYP-Annual Yearly Progress" requirements that make potential teachers take a second look at the teaching profession. Granted, all of the assessments and movements above have a degree of validity, but what is the true underlying factor of these paramount changes in education. Is it to stabilize or push a political platform, receive more money for state education department coffers, or to make your state or district look good by having a high score or ranking among other systems? Educational movements should be about simply helping our youth to learn in an educationally sound, and safe environment. The goal should be to make our students feel good about their achievements, and about themselves.

Are our tests really designed to evaluate and assess student outcomes or are they designed to devalue and stifle bright futures? I will be the first one to agree that assessments and tests are necessary, but they don't have to take the place of good "old fashioned" teaching in the classroom. When control of the classroom is given back to the teachers, I believe that we will see wonderful and progressive results from our students. After all, the people who have designed these tests, and are strongly pushing these movements were taught in good "old fashioned" classrooms. It's my guess that they learned a lot, because they are smart enough to make money from their testing ideas and materials.

Education is constantly evolving and so are our youth. It is true that we must make drastic changes to our educational system; however, a little rational thinking would be a welcomed part of the change. Whatever we do as a society will either have a positive or a negative impact on our future. Many of our world's greatest leaders would have probably been discouraged had they been subjected to the stresses of these types of tests.

My home State of Georgia has made great strides in creating a statewide "Quality Core Curriculum", and by developing its most recent improvement, which is the "Georgia Performance Standards", but problems still exists. One problem is that each teacher may teach at a different pace and impart instruction at different degrees of difficulty, from classroom to classroom. The next problem is that not all schools have the same textbooks. Another problem is that emphasis made on a particular topic by one teacher may not be made by the other. I wish someone would explain to me, how in the world do you expect all students to learn the same thing, at the same time, using different textbooks, in different school systems? The answer is you can't, without some type of uniform teaching requirements.

I have witnessed children literally cry and shake nervously because they were frightened because of the tests that they were required to take. They have been drilled and drilled time and time again, and told that if they don't pass their tests, they will not be promoted to the next grade. Some teachers and administrators were also concerned because the scores of students who are receiving Special Education services were calculated with those students' scores who are receiving education from the general curriculum. This complicates the matter even more. It is not clear to many how tests are to be administered to these students. Is it supposed to be read to them, or not? The instructions need to be clear and concise across the board. It is difficult to measure a student's achievement by using a single evaluation instrument. Our children are already facing enough struggles as it is, and now they are being subjected to even more. When we spend all of our time constantly administering these tests, there is little time left in the classroom, for our children to learn.

Teachers and administrators are feeling the same type of stress all across our country. Many of them are saying that they don't have the opportunity to effectively teach their students because of so many testing requirements. There are others who have also stated that student behavior and nonchalant attitudes are a factor in why student test scores are not where they need to be. If this is true, then why are so many teachers being put in front of the "firing squad" and taking the rap for students who don't even care if they pass or not? My reasoning for entering the educational field was and still is to help others succeed. I have gone, and will continue to go beyond the call of duty to make sure that students are given every opportunity to succeed, but to what degree they want to succeed is up to them.

I understand that my views on education are my views, but I felt compelled to write this narrative because I can sense the pain and distress that many of my colleagues are feeling on a daily basis. I thank God that I was raised by parents who taught me not to complain, without offering a solution to the problem. What is the solution? The person with that answer would undoubtedly receive the Nobel Peace Prize for bringing peace of mind to students, parents, teachers, administrators, Boards of Education, and communities all across our country. The reality is that there is no one solution to the problem. However, we must begin by suggesting some.

Possible Solutions

1. Allow teachers who are on the front lines, to regain control of their classroom.
2. Develop system-wide evaluation tools for students within a system that reflects what is actually being taught.
3. Give the control of a school back to capable administrators, who have the teacher's and the student's best interest in mind and not their own.
4. Encourage positive parental participation and unbiased support of their children and teachers.
5. Hold everyone accountable for student learning and progress, including the student.
6. Teachers need to write their elected officials often, and keep them informed of the effects that the laws that they make are having on their lives and the lives of their students.
7. Encourage more emphasis on character education and institute a time of true reflection for students.
8. Parents should monitor what their children wear to school and what they watch on T.V./ Movies/DVD and what they listen to as well.
9. Ensure that the entire community does their part in making a difference in the lives of our youth.
10. Start a youth leadership program in your community.

   If all else fails, pray! (We might want to do this one first.)

In conclusion, education will change if we can collectively agree to change our own and sometimes isolated ways of thinking, to reflect what is actually best for our students and empower our administrators, teachers, parents, and community with the tools to make the necessary improvements.

Okay, as I promised, I am through venting regarding educational issues and now we can get down to the business of getting your youth leadership program started. Roll up your sleeves and make sure that you have an extra case of coffee. Just kidding!

Step One

Survey The Citizens Of The Community

Public Opinion Of Youth Program

It is imperative that the public's opinion is included in the process of establishing a youth program. Educating the public on your desires and needs will enable them to become more actively involved in helping you accomplish your mission. Strong allies are needed to help spread the message of empowering our youth to be the best that they can be. Public opinion, in my opinion, is better sought in advance, than voiced later, in a negative and uncensored manner. It can be the life or the demise of any effort to start a program.

It is important to talk about the possibilities of the program to key community leaders and ask them for an off the record or on the record comment about the viability of such a program. You would be surprised at what you can find out early on about the general views of the members of the community. Please do not be discouraged if you hear negative opinions, because they are only opinions. However, you should not discount the validity of those opinions, but you should do your own investigation to see if they are indeed valid. If they are, make the necessary corrections and move forward, and if they aren't, move forward. Remember, some negative opinions stem from those who wished that they had thought of your idea to start a youth program.

Public opinion is often heard loud and clear during election time, and most often that voice is from only a small percentage of actual registered voters. Use the same strategy by recruiting powerful (not controversial) voices in the community who will support you and your efforts to start a community youth program.

Notes

The Type Of Program For The Community

There are countless numbers of combinations for success of community youth programs. A program in one community may work brilliantly, but that same program in a different community may not be as successful. For example, a "train the young farmer program" would be a great fit for a rural area in South Georgia, but it may not be, for someone who lives in downtown Los Angeles, California. There is some truth to what people in a community may say when they make comments such as: "We do things this way around here; or the nerve of those people, they don't know our community like we do," especially when new ideas and inevitable change is at their door steps.

Whether you are a member of a particular community or not, you can tell very quickly whether an idea will set well with the community by the responses you get. Please don't misunderstand me, and please don't be afraid to make things happen for the better, but it is very important that you do some very careful planning and research and recognize the signs that often blink brightly when they display the word(s) "It Fits" or "It Doesn't Fit". However, do not give up with just one attempt. Have you ever tried to make something fit, but it just would not, then you tried it later, and it did fit? Some youth programs are just that way.

Just as cars have blinking lights (turn signal lights) that indicates to the people in the cars around you that you are about to turn a certain direction, the signals you receive from your community should indicate to you whether or not you should stay the course or change directions. Turn signals do not indicate that you are about to stop, but that you are about to turn, so don't stop, but be flexible and go in the direction that is best for the youth and the community as a whole.

Notes

The Opinions of Local Elected Officials

Whatever you do, please ensure that you acknowledge your local elected officials by engaging them in the process as well. They can be a great resource for funding, building space, and connecting you to people who may be able to assist you. Although many local governments are faced with unfunded mandates and infrastructure woes, most of them are willing to help. Elected officials, who are charged with spearheading youth leadership or other community programs, should take full advantage of networking with other local officials and the community, to bring them on board.

There are cases where political divisions exist in a community. You should be aware that partisan politics and attitudes might interfere with your progress. Unfortunately, this situation is often brought into the equation. A passive attitude toward these types of situations could interrupt your journey toward creating a successful program and your train toward success could very quickly become derailed. This does not have to happen to your efforts, especially if you remain in a neutral non-partisan position.

What I am about to say is not meant to be controversial, but it is something that you should know. Please let me enlighten you to the fact that all elected officials are not in office for the same reasons. Some have personal agendas, which motivated them to seek public office. However, there are others who are there to serve for the good of the community. Your ultimate goal is find common ground amongst the elected officials of a community, and use that common ground to benefit your efforts. Express to them that it is okay to agree to disagree, but there should be enough similar goals for the future of the youth and the community that out weigh the dissimilar ones.

Notes

Empowering The Next Generation

Assistance From Community Service Agencies

Community service agencies possess a wealth of experience, resources, and personnel that may be helpful to you in starting a successful youth leadership program. Most service agencies have longevity in the community, and are very well known and respected. These agencies may be funded by a combination of private donations, and local, state, and federal dollars. Some have specific missions that they are required to accomplish, which may prove to be very helpful to your cause.

There are agencies that return unused funds back to the government every year because very few programs applied to receive the designated funds. Believe it or not, some agency heads have reported that they have tried to let the community know that certain funds were available, but sometimes they were not as successful at their attempts as they hoped they would be. My advice to you is to exhaust any and all opportunities to request funds for your program. Don't be embarrassed if you are denied funding by one agency or five agencies, because sooner or later someone will see the vision you see.

Government and private agencies and foundations are also a great source for help in getting your program started. A brief Internet search of these agencies may also prove to be beneficial. Some people are discouraged because of the amount of effort it takes to search for these agencies. Others are discouraged by the amount of required paperwork associated with receiving certain funds, and those two groups are the people who usually give up. Take your time and follow the necessary guidelines set forth by these agencies, and increase your chances of being funded. Persistence pays off, so ask, and more than likely you will receive.

Notes

Local School Personnel Opinions And Suggestions

School system superintendents, principals, counselors, teachers, and support staff are all valuable resources. These people are representatives of the community, and they are in direct contact with the youth of the community, sometimes, for more hours than the parents themselves. As an educator, I know what the problems of the community are because I see and hear it straight from the source each and every day. These officials may not be able to divulge personal student information, but they can be a great resource for you in general terms.

Schedule some time to talk with the principal to find out what problems are occurring on campus. The same problems occurring on campus are often similar to the problems in the community. Schedule a meeting with the teachers and ask them to list three to five of the major problems that they are having in the classroom. Talk with the support staff, which in most cases is comprised of people from the heart of the community. These people could write a book about the needs of their community and it would probably become a bestseller. Take advantage of these free and readily accessible resources within your school system.

Most states produce a school system report card for each school system in that state. The report card provides information about the school's overall performance, as it relates to standardized test scores, absenteeism, and school dropout rates, just to name a few. This data may be used as proof that certain problems do exist in the community. Usually, this information can be found on a state's Department of Education website. As a result of your research of this data, you may decide to incorporate some goals that address these and other important community and youth related issues.

Notes

_____

_____

_____

_____

_____

_____

_____

_____

_____

_____

_____

_____

_____

_____

_____

_____

_____

_____

_____

_____

_____

_____

_____

_____

Opinions From The Youth Of The Community

It would be a travesty of justice, if we didn't consult with the very population of people that we are trying to help, which are our youth. Some have called the youth of today, the "lost generation", but have not offered any help to find them. Even though many of our youth are headed toward a path that leads to nowhere, they are not a lost cause. In fact, most of the youth that I come in contact with on a daily basis are headed down the right path. However, their successes are often overshadowed by the actions of a few bad apples. It is up to us to provide consistent and meaningful intervention when and where it is needed, and starting a youth program is the beginning of that intervention. We need to ask them their views about the importance of a youth program in their community. If you can get them to buy in early, that is one obstacle that you will have overcome.

Upon the establishment of your program, you will have the opportunity to work with all types of youth. You will soon find out that the youth in your program can be very persuasive in justifying their actions and arguing their points of view, but you as a mentor and a leader should possess some of the skills necessary to help trim away the unhealthy parts of those apples (views and actions) and salvage the good.

The youth in your program will look to you to provide the expertise necessary to help them find common ground. Don't worry about being an expert in everything, because no one is. If you are not an expert there is still hope for you. I am sure that you can find one in your community who is willing to help you. Most of the time, they are just waiting for you to ask for their help. Your task is to find those experts and learn as much as you can from them and continue to impart that new knowledge to the youth in your program. The youth of your community are your most valuable assets. If you neglect them and fail to request and consider their opinions, there is no doubt in my mind that your program will be missing an important piece of the puzzle.

Notes

_____

_____

_____

_____

_____

_____

_____

_____

_____

_____

_____

_____

_____

_____

_____

_____

_____

_____

_____

_____

_____

_____

Notes

Step Two

Evaluate The Need Using Statistical Data

Teen Pregnancy and Sexually Transmitted Diseases

Teen Pregnancy and Sexually Transmitted Diseases are ever increasing problems in communities across our country and around the world. From the early to the late 1990's, statistical reports indicated that teen pregnancy rates were on a decline. However, recent reports indicate that the teen pregnancy rate has begun to increase. Evaluate the situation in your own community by visiting the local health department. I understand that they may not be able to share the names of the girls with you, but they will be able to share statistical information and any brochures that they may have on hand.

Teen pregnancy is still a problem in our schools and in our communities. This important data and a solution to correct the problem will solidify your case with a variety of community stakeholders. I am of the opinion that every teen pregnancy case is a potential sexually transmitted disease case. When you present your case to the powers that be, don't be afraid to respectfully tell them like it is. There is no time to waste, especially when this epidemic is contributing to why people remain in poverty. The sad fact about this entire ordeal is that it is preventable. What is your opinion?

It is up to everyone in the community to take action against this preventable problem. Yes, it is a problem, especially when the mothers are just children themselves. Many boys and girls are irresponsible and not ready to accept the responsibility of being a full-fledged mother or father. That is why we must do all that we can do to encourage them to wait until they are ready, and able to take on that responsibility.

Notes

_____

_____

_____

_____

_____

_____

_____

_____

_____

_____

_____

_____

_____

_____

_____

_____

_____

_____

_____

_____

_____

_____

_____

Drugs, Alcohol, And Tobacco Use

I have coined the phrase for the use of drugs, alcohol, and tobacco by our youth, as the acquaintance with the "three deadly plagues". There are countless numbers of websites and print literature that discuss the effects that these plagues have on our generation of youth. Gather as much data as you can, regarding the use of these substances by talking with your local police department and health department officials. They know first hand of what our communities are facing, and they know what impact these devices are having on our youth.

It is easy, if you want to see it, just look out your kitchen window in some communities and see a drug deal in progress. I know what I am talking about, because I rode by our local park and saw a drug deal in progress, and I was disgusted at what I saw. Your effective evaluation and implementation of solutions will help to eradicate or at least help to reduce the use and misuse of drugs, alcohol, and tobacco in your community. Use your statistical data to drive home your case for an immediate youth leadership program.

There is a wealth of resources available to you to share with your young participants, once your program is up and running. You will be amazed at the differing views that you will get when this topic is discussed. You must also be aware that you just might have a drug user and a drug dealer in your program. With that said, you may only have one opportunity to make a positive impact, so do the best you can to offer a better alternative. You have to keep in mind that the dealer or user may actually be in your program to get the help they need to get their lives back on track. Always keep your eyes opened for these types of opportunities to help.

Notes

_____

_____

_____

_____

_____

_____

_____

_____

_____

_____

_____

_____

_____

_____

_____

_____

_____

_____

_____

_____

_____

_____

_____

_____

_____

School Absenteeism And School Drop Out Rate

Which comes first the egg or the chicken? Which comes first the problems at home or the problems at school? Just imagine how far advanced we would be if we knew the answers to all of life's puzzling questions. There are numerous reasons why students are excessively absent from school. Some of those reasons may be related to abuse at home, drug use, and other criminal activity.

Conducting a survey of your own community can be very effective. Use local data, along with state and national statistics to help drive home your point to local leaders. Chronic absenteeism often leads to students dropping out of school. It is also important to gather current data from the school systems in your community. This data often times will shed a bit of light on a variety of factors that contribute to truancy and school dropout rates.

Students who drop out of school have plenty of time on their hands to get involved in all sorts of mischief and illegal behavior. The longer they stay out of school, the harder it is to get them to return. Many of them get a taste of freedom and independence. Freedom and independence are both good things to have, but at the right time. If the youth in your community are free and independent and uneducated, that is a recipe for disaster. To me, that means that they have no sense of what their limitations are, and more times than not, that leads to possible criminal activity. Express your concerns to your local governing authorities and make certain that they understand that your program will try and help reduce instances of school absenteeism and school dropout. It is also a good idea to present some type of evidence of what you have already done, without their help, and stress how much more you can do with their help.

Notes

_____

_____

_____

_____

_____

_____

_____

_____

_____

_____

_____

_____

_____

_____

_____

_____

_____

_____

_____

_____

_____

_____

Active Youth Probation Cases

Researching active youth probation cases is one way to find out who your target population might be. It is true that not all youth who violate the law are habitual, but it will give you information about who, and specifics about what, when, where, and how these crimes or incidences of breaking the law occurred. It is understood that much of the information about an actual person may not be available, and that is okay, because you don't need the names of the individuals; you need the statistical information.

Once you have established your program, notify the probation officer or office in your city or county and ask them to make your information available to those who are on probation. You should not be weary of having these individuals as a part of your program because all of our children need positive attention. Many of these youngsters will probably jump at the opportunity to do whatever it takes to please the judge and their probation officer. In the process of trying to please those individuals, they might hear, see, or do something that might ignite an interest in the program for what it offers them, and not for the other motives of pleasing someone else.

Many of these youth are accustomed to receiving extrinsic motivators; those motivators that offer some type of a tangible reward, such as money, drugs, or other material things. Your goal is to ignite a fire within the hearts of these individuals that will cause them to do certain things because it is just the right thing to do. When these youth begin to feel an intrinsic motivation toward participating in your program; half of your work will already be done for you. The name of this game is encouragement and empowerment and it doesn't make a difference if your participant is on probation or not, they still need that bit of encouragement.

Notes

_____

_____

_____

_____

_____

_____

_____

_____

_____

_____

_____

_____

_____

_____

_____

_____

_____

_____

_____

_____

_____

_____

Community Involvement

Community involvement is such a broad term, and it needs to be. It is very difficult to narrow down any one aspect of being involved in one's community. Statistical information about community involvement may already be available at your City Hall or at your local Chamber of Commerce. Many times these agencies are aware of what the needs of the community are and most are more than willing to give you information so that they may have your help to meet these needs.

Effective evaluation of this need can lead to more community involvement. A youth program can increase involvement. Communities often have a need for help with upcoming events, such as annual festivals, visits from special individuals, or the recognition of a milestone in the community. Some communities keep participation data, such as names, addresses, and phone numbers, for the ease of contacting potential volunteers for future events.

Other types of community events may be related to keeping the community safe, with programs such as "Neighborhood Watch". Upon collection of statistical data, share with the community about the important role that every citizen of a city, county, parish, district, or region plays in ensuring the success of the community. Personal experience has taught me that some of these citizens may need a little priming to get started.

I am of the belief that most citizens do care about their communities, however, a great many of them leave it up to others to do the bulk of the work. You may provide encouragement to citizens by expressing to them that their contributions are of monumental importance, and the intrinsic satisfaction gained from being involved in one's community is immeasurable. Obtaining a list of those who are already involved in your community might be beneficial to the start-up of your youth program.

Notes

_____

_____

_____

_____

_____

_____

_____

_____

_____

_____

_____

_____

_____

_____

_____

_____

_____

_____

_____

_____

_____

_____

_____

_____

Gang Activity

The statistical results from gang activities alone can be enough to encourage the development of a Youth Program. It is no secret that gang activity is on the rise, and so are crimes associated with these types of activities. Local, state, and federal law enforcement agencies have created special units, whose main focus is reducing gang activities. Such agencies possess detailed statistical information regarding the types and names of gangs, and whether they exist in your community.

These agencies may also be able to provide you with information regarding gang related crimes in the community, as well as state and federal crime statistics. You may request information by writing a letter to the person in charge of the Gang Unit, or you may schedule an appointment to personally speak to a member of the unit. I would not encourage anyone to take matters into their own hands and confront gang members face to face, because this can be very dangerous. Gang members don't care whether or not you're trying to help the community. The fact of the matter is you and your youth program may pose a threat to their gang operations.

Most gangs prey on people with low self-esteems, and these are the very ones that your youth program can target. Gangs also prey on youth who think that they have to prove something to themselves and society. The spectrum is long and wide, regarding the types of youth that are attracted by and to gangs.

Often times you may be a target of intimidation by gangs in your community, but my advice is to report any harassment to the appropriate authorities and stay focused on the mission at hand. The presentation of statistical data from gang activities in your community and how your program would address this issue is of paramount importance.

Notes

_____

_____

_____

_____

_____

_____

_____

_____

_____

_____

_____

_____

_____

_____

_____

_____

_____

_____

_____

_____

_____

_____

_____

_____

Step Three

Communicate The Need To Local Community Leaders

Focus of Program

Would you support a program if someone came to you and did not have a clear focus? I may not be there to hear your answer, but I am guessing that your answer is no. It is imperative that you have a clear and defined focus for your program. You should prepare yourself by answering as many anticipated questions from community leaders as you possibly can, because I can assure you that you will receive a wide array of them.

Establishing a clear vision statement and mission statement are two ways to help you reiterate your focus. Your vision statement lets possible supporters know what your expected outcomes are going to be and your mission statement helps define the manner in which you hope to accomplish the vision. It has been said, that without a vision, the people perish. I am telling you that without a clear focus, your efforts will become very blurry and then your hopes of a youth program could possibly perish.

You also should be aware that not everyone wants you to succeed, and they are going to test you at every level of progression. You have to do your homework before you enter into any type of venue to discuss your program. Often times, questions are intentionally asked to delay your progress. Be Prepared! Be Ready! Be Sharp! Hold Yourself Together!

It is important to appeal to community leaders individually and collectively, and you should be aware of each leader's position regarding your program ideas and your request for help. Outlining your program's goals and objectives are other ways that will help you to clearly express your purpose.

Notes

Funding And Budgeting Concerns

Money does not grow on trees, but you can find it in the pockets of community stakeholders. Funding and budgeting concerns are often the cause of the demise of youth programs before they are even started. Some communities just don't see why they should allocate funds for a youth program. It is your duty to cause a paradigm shift, in their minds, so that the money will begin to flow. It is nearly impossible to do that, without first knowing how much money your program is going to need.

Starting a youth program is similar to starting a business, in the respect that you must prepare a budget and create a business plan. Your business plan may be created in phases, as to show that you can accomplish an objective of a stated goal, with a certain amount of funding. This just might open the door to some funding, even if it is not all of the funding at one time. Remember, you are going to look in more than one direction for funding. Stakeholders need to know how much they are going to have to give and how often, and for how long. Your program's business plan should include information regarding the cost of rent or leasing a facility, utilities, insurance, staff, training and travel, supplies, and food, etc. If you are granted the use of a facility at no charge, your focus should be concentrated on those other issues, which are all important.

Whatever happens, please don't give up. You may have to do a little traveling around your state, other states, and even to Washington, D.C. to find funding for your program. I have flown to Washington several times to ask for funds for a variety of projects that our city needed help with. Your Congressmen and Senators are in office to serve you, and you should take advantage of the many services they have to offer. Don't be afraid to ask, because if you are, someone else may get what was meant for you.

Notes

_____

_____

_____

_____

_____

_____

_____

_____

_____

_____

_____

_____

_____

_____

_____

_____

_____

_____

_____

_____

_____

_____

_____

_____

Oversight and Staffing of Program

Who's in charge? That is a question you should already have the answer too before you approach local community stakeholders. Those who will be responsible for the operational aspects of the program need to be up front and center. Successful organizations have obtained success by effective planning and organizing. It is of the utmost importance that the program's organizational structure comes by way of long hours of planning. Planning ensures that your objectives will be clear and easily understood.

Have you ever considered the value of volunteers? If you haven't, now is the time, because volunteers can be a valuable resource to any program. The more volunteers you have, the more possible supporters will feel at ease regarding the sustainability of your program. There are many factors that go into the equation of starting a successful youth program. One of those factors is whether or not the program can be sustained with volunteers, if the need arises. Supporters want to know that their contributions will not be given in vain. In other words, they want to know that the program will continue, even if future financial support is lacking.

Continually explore solutions to staffing, because just as the ocean has a high tide and a low tide, from time to time, your program may experience similar changes. Complacency can be your worst enemy, especially when it catches you unaware. Create a waiting list with the names of individuals with an expressed interested in serving on your staff, as possible volunteers. You should also have someone who can take charge, in the event that you are absent or no longer can operate the program. This will ensure that your program will remain in operation for years to come.

Notes

Target Population

Where will you be when you get where you are going? Who are you trying to reach? Why are you trying to reach these individuals? You are sure to be asked these questions by local leaders. If you have truly done your homework using the information from previous sections of this guide, you probably have already realized who your target population is and where they are located. Just in case you have missed the mark, I'll go into further detail.

Local leaders like to get the most "bang for their buck", for the lack of better words. Most supporters take pride in knowing that their contributions have returned positive dividends. Choosing a population that is in need of the help can make your job a lot easier than just choosing a population where there is not a clear need. The target population is bound to be located in somebody's Ward or District. Getting an endorsement from that district's representative may very well make your burden a little lighter and your day a little brighter. Just be sure to clearly state whom your target population is and where they are located.

It never hurts to have a representation of your target population present at the meeting, especially when you first bring this topic before your governing authority or board. Use a bit of caution, and prepare the group, by providing instructions on how to behave in a public meeting. You may say that they already know how to behave, but I am saying that you should make sure that they do. Many of the individuals in your target population probably have never attended a city council meeting or any meeting of this nature. Take my advice and have a mock meeting to prepare your group for what might be said at a meeting. If you do this, you will not be made ashamed at your first meeting.

Notes

_____
_____
_____
_____
_____
_____
_____
_____
_____
_____
_____
_____
_____
_____
_____
_____
_____
_____
_____
_____
_____
_____
_____

Location of Program/Implementation Guidelines

Where will your program be housed? That is the million-dollar question. Program location depends on a plethora of factors. One factor has to do with whether or not you have adequate financial backing to be located where you want to be located. Another factor has to do with whether or not you have been offered a facility free of charge or for minimal cost.

Safety is always a major consideration when you are considering a location for a facility. It will be advantageous to have a facility in the community where the problem or issues are. On the other hand, it may be more advantageous to allow youth to experience what it is like attend the program in other environments. Community leaders are well aware of the demographics of their respective cities and their knowledge of this may be to your advantage.

The ultimate goal is to provide the most effective intervention, using the most effective practices, in the most effective environment. You may be surprised at the fact that some community stakeholders may began vying for the program to be located in their area of the community. This is good, especially if the competition is healthy, and fair. It is up to you to ensure that it is, and you can do this by making it a citywide event, if it comes to this. However, don't be disappointed if no one competes for your program.

In the process of establishing the location, it is very important that you multitask and create a timeline for program implementation, as well. Give yourself enough time to complete all the tasks at hand. If you have thought about starting your program first, then figuring out the rest later, think again. It is better for you to extend the time for a grand opening, than for you to have a quick grand opening and grand closing at the same time.

Notes

Evaluation and Tracking Measures

The leaders of great programs can easily explain to you why their program is great. As painstaking as it may be, data collection may be the lifeblood of your program. We live in a data driven society, where people want to see results. Those who offer their support for your program want to know whether or not the program is helping youth and the community. My advice to you is to keep accurate and up to date records on each and every participant in your program.

Always keep parental contact information, school information, such as about absences, and grades, etc. Also keep information about the youth's participation in your program. Share these important methods of evaluation and tracking with community leaders and supporters. Effective tracking can be of great help to your program, especially if you are considering applying for grants. Grant raters look for data collected over a period of time, because it gives them what they need to make a more informed decision about the denial or approval of grant funds.

It is good practice to keep any information that you have regarding your program and participants, for a few years. Remember, your goal is for these young leaders to further their education and become successful contributors to society. Your accurate records could serve as evidence of their participation in your program, which may mean the difference between a youth getting a scholarship, or a job, or not.

It is also great for providing verification, just in case one of your former members becomes famous, or even becomes the next president of the United States. This is not as farfetched as it sounds. If this occurs, your program will probably never have to worry about funding again. If not, having a youth program makes the difference anyway.

Notes

_____

_____

_____

_____

_____

_____

_____

_____

_____

_____

_____

_____

_____

_____

_____

_____

_____

_____

_____

_____

_____

_____

_____

Step Four

Design Your Program And Curriculum

Choose The Right Curriculum

Youth programs that operate without a curriculum are taking risks that I wouldn't be willing to take, nor should you. A sound curriculum offers structure for the facilitator/instructor and the youth themselves, and without it; disaster is imminent. Your program's curriculum is simply a guide used to steer the youth and your program in the right direction. It is a course of study. Most of us should remember our teachers in school following their system's curriculum and preparing their lesson plans each day. I remember watching my teachers refer to what they had written for a particular lesson. They used their plans to guide them in delivering instruction to the class.

A curriculum is a road map that guides you in the right direction. However, it is as equally important to know what kind of curriculum you are going to use as well. Just having a curriculum for the sake of having one is no good either. An effective curriculum will aid in meeting the various goals and objectives that you want to achieve. If you have a problem choosing the right curriculum, it is perfectly acceptable to write your own.

Keep in mind your vision and your mission when writing your curriculum. You may also choose to use different aspects of several different curriculums to form what is ideal for your program. Whatever you do, please don't allow yourself to become bogged down with a curriculum that doesn't work. If it doesn't work for your program, go ahead and cut your losses and find something that does work. Also, make sure that you choose a curriculum that is fun as well as educational.

Notes

Establish Staff Responsibilities

It is a must that you are very clear about the kind of people you hire to help you operate your youth program. Successful programs hire positive-minded, energetic, proactive, and self-motivated people to help with the execution of the program. A clear set of personnel procedures and guidelines must also be established. An organizational chart should be created so that employees/volunteers understand the chain of command and where they are located on the chain.

Clear and precise responsibilities should be explained before and upon hiring program personnel. It is also important to conduct background checks on everyone associated with your program, because safety is concern number one. I have found that it is a good practice to schedule meetings with staff to listen to their concerns and share your concerns as well. Each member of your staff should understand their role and remember that they are important to the overall process of effectively training a generation of youth.

You should make every effort to have fun, while accomplishing the mission. The attitudes of you and your staff are contagious, and the youth of your program will pick up on any dissention in a heartbeat. Remember, your goal is to positively shape the behavior of the youth in your community. If you do not have a positive attitude, you are sending the wrong message, and those wrong messages could easily destroy your program.

More importantly, those wrong messages could destroy any progress that you may have made concerning your youth. The ultimate goal is to be a true professional, so that the youth of your program will have a positive example, in which to follow. Remember that all eyes are on you and your staff.

Carl L. Camon, Ed.S

Notes

_____

_____

_____

_____

_____

_____

_____

_____

_____

_____

_____

_____

_____

_____

_____

_____

_____

_____

_____

_____

_____

Criteria For Youth Entry Into The Program

Every youth program should have criteria for entry. Criteria for entry in some programs are as different as night and day. Your criteria should depend on several factors, such as, the length of your program, the amount of space you have, the amount of staff you have, the amount of time you have, and the amount of support you have. If your program is 6 weeks long and you have several program rotations a year, you may be able to have a smaller number of participants at any given time. However, if you only have a few rotations a year, then you may want to accept as many participants into the program as you can.

The size of your facility plays a major role in the amount of participants you can have in your program. The size of your staff is also a very important factor because you have to ensure that your youth are adequately supervised. Some programs are granted the use of facilities only certain times of the year, in those cases you may want to maximize the number of youth that can participate in your program at one time. There are other factors such as the youth's willingness to participate in your program.

In our youth program, we set an age criteria of 10 – 17 years old, but you may want to set your own requirements for entry. Remember, your goal is to reach as many youth as you can, especially those who are a part of your target population. Smaller cities may not have a problem with the number of youth who can participate in their program at any given time. Some smaller programs have more lenient criteria and they may accept as many youth as they can get, within a particular age bracket. Larger cities, however, have larger numbers of youth, and the program criteria may be stricter, because of the numbers.

Notes

Establish The Duration of Each Class/Session

The duration of each class of participants should be clearly established. Will you hold your program in the summer, fall, winter, or spring, or year around, and for what length of time? Some programs are held in the summer, because of the convenience of having a "ready made" group of participants. The average summer program lasts from four to six hours a day, for two to four weeks.

During the school year, some programs are held after school for specified periods of time. You have the flexibility of establishing your own times, because after all, it will be your program and you will know what you can or cannot handle. Most parents begin looking for activities for their children to do, even before the summer break officially begins. Parents love summer youth programs, because many of them provide opportunities for their children to stay mentally and physically involved.

You should be aware that there will be some parents who will try and use your youth program as a babysitting or daycare service. You should be firm in adhering to established requirements, such as drop-off and pick-up times and the age limit requirements. Create written documents explaining all applicable aspects of the program to the participant and their parents, and require each of them to sign the document indicating that they understand. This will help to ensure that your program is not a childcare service, but a youth leadership program.

Occasionally, you may want to invite all of the youth of a community to your program for refreshments. Keep in mind that your current participants will soon graduate, and you'll have a ready-made class that will be familiar about your program. Entice them with cookies and soda; I'm sorry, cookies and milk.

Notes

Choose A Name For The Program

I am sure that you have heard the saying, "You never get a second chance to make a first impression". Even though program names don't rank at the top of most contributors list of important requirements, a relevant name is important. Before choosing a name, you should consider the environment that you're in. Will the name flow with the community in which your program is located?

For example, if you name your youth program The Young Vikings, because you attended Viking High School, but the facility is located on the side of town where the rival Wildcats are located, you just might have a problem. You may make the decision to choose a name that is relevant to the mission at hand or one that has some other significant relationship to community. Many programs are named after benefactors, elected officials, or someone who may be highly respected in the community.

Whatever you do, please do not choose a controversial name, because it will do more harm than good. Your youth program should always remain on neutral ground, especially when you're seeking help from a wide range of supporters. Holding a community wide contest and asking for the citizens of your community to submit a name for the program is also a great way to choose a name.

Remember, ensure that the name has relevance. Why relevance? Everything that you do on behalf of the youth of your community must have some degree of relevance. You are training the next leaders of your community, city, state, nation, and world. They need to know from the very beginning of their involvement in your program, That everything will have relevance. Most importantly, they need to understand that not only is your program's name relevant, but that all of their names are relevant, as well.

Notes

Create By-Laws For The Program

The creation or the adoption of official by-laws for your program adds credibility. By-Laws are official rules that regulate the operation of your program. By-Laws often state what officers are required to be a part of the program. Officers, such as the Chairman, the President, the Vice-President, the Secretary, and the Treasurer are all official positions that may be found listed in the by-laws of a program.

The adoption of by-laws may help your program combat various challenges that may arise, especially as it relates to questions dealing with leadership and authority. Each officer and member will better understand their role and stay within the confines of their role as well. Grant providers often look at the by-laws of programs, because it helps them understand how and by whom the program is governed. It is important to remember that millions of grant dollars are at stake and sometimes the competition can be fierce. Any thing that you or your program has that gives you an edge over the competition is always helpful.

Supporters feel more secure knowing that their money is going to benefit an organization or program that has a reasonably acceptable structure, of which by-laws often help make up. You may use an attorney to create a set of by-laws based on the mission of your program, or you may search the Internet for examples. The latter choice is free. Please be aware that Internet examples are just that, and you should not copy anyone's by-laws and claim them for your own, without written permission, but you may use the examples as a guide. Also, allow your youth to help create the by-laws of your program. Their participation solidifies their commitment to the program and holds them accountable as well.

Notes

Step Five

Establish Positive Relationships With Community Partners

Create A Stakeholder Contact Log

Do you know where I put that phone number? Did he give me a business card? What was that lady's name that offered to help us with our program? The above questions are a few that I have asked, especially when I was trying to find some very important information that I needed. You may have other questions that you have asked similar to mine. To avoid these questions, delays in time, and missed deadlines, it is important that you keep accurate contact information.

Create a contact log on your computer and at least two paper copies and store in a safe place. You can add or delete data, and community stakeholder information as necessary. It is also important to keep regular contact with the agencies on your contact log, because these agencies often change the requirements for submitting request for assistance. Also, your continued contact keeps your youth program on the minds of agencies and businesses that are in positions to help, because these community partners often have additional resources, in the way of finances, and access to other possible agencies that may be interested in providing assistance to your program, as well.

You may also use the vast amount of resources located on the Internet, in order to build your contact list. The Internet may provide you and your program with access to hundreds of agencies that are located around the world. It is important to explore resources outside of your community or city. Some agencies provide help on a global scale, and if your youth leadership program is located on earth, then it may be eligible.

Notes

Build Relationships With The Community

Community stakeholders are those businesses, organizations, agencies, households, churches, and individuals who have a stake in the community. You should make every effort to notify each one of those entities at some point during the development phases of your program. Work to build and strengthen positive relationships throughout the life of your program.

Community stakeholders often seek out worthy programs in which to make their annual contributions. Effective and continual communication with stakeholders opens the door to your program and increases the likelihood that it will make it onto the list of potential recipients. The fact is that these businesses really do have a stake in the community. They understand that their contributions will benefit them and the community in a positive way. For example, if a contributor's donation helps to prevent a child from joining a gang, because that child participated in a gang prevention program, then that contributor as well as the community benefits. One less gang member may equate to one less murder, robbery, rape, or larceny case.

Convey to reluctant contributors that their donation is an investment in the future of their community and in the lives of future leaders of the community as well. It is important to be persistent, but not over bearing in your approach. Community stakeholders are all too familiar with what is occurring around them. Your task is to ensure that they clearly understand that your program can make a difference in the community. Convey to them the direct relationship that exists between them and the youth that they see everyday. I believe that effective communication will yield positive results.

Notes

Formulate A List Of Facilitators, Speakers, And Experts

Perhaps you will know your program better than anyone else, but always remember that you do not know it all. I founded the Mayor's Youth Leadership Institute of Ray City, and I know the program inside and out, but I have a confession; I don't know it all. Over the years I have relied on so many people to help make our program the best that it could be. I have invited Legislators, Judges, Lobbyist, Mayors, Chamber of Commerce Executives, City Council Members, Doctors, Lawyers, Health Department Directors, College Professors, and Military Men and Women, just to name a few.

I could not have provided the expertise that these men and women brought to our program. There was never an occasion when I had to force a facilitator or speaker to visit our program. Every time that I made a phone request or an in - person request, the answer was always yes. Of course there were scheduling conflicts at times, but the answer was still always yes. The experts that I invited knew about their respective fields, and most of them were anxious to share that knowledge with others.

Devise a list of speakers from every imaginable career field that you can think of, and make an initial contact with them, and inform them of your program. Also, be sure to let them know that you are looking for volunteers to come and share with your program participants. Be sure to find out if there are any charges associated with their visit. Most agencies don't charge for visiting with non-profit or community related programs. On occasion, our program would purchase a fruit basket and give it to the speaker as a token of our appreciation, especially if our speaker traveled a great distance to be with our youth. You do what is best to show your appreciation, and be aware that anything you do may help to strengthen that relationship.

Notes

_____

_____

_____

_____

_____

_____

_____

_____

_____

_____

_____

_____

_____

_____

_____

_____

_____

_____

_____

_____

_____

_____

_____

_____

Establish Positive Relationships With Local Media

The local media can be your best friend or your worst enemy. Make friends with local media, such as, local newspapers, radio stations, and television stations. These media outlets can get the message out to the masses one hundred times faster than you can. Your goal is for people to know about the program and local media can make that happen. There should be a designated spokesperson that knows the program and one who knows how to communicate effectively with others.

Contact local news agencies and schedule some time to sit down and talk face to face. Share with them the important aspects of your program and why it is needed in the community. You may also want to have something in writing, so as to not stray away from the message that you are trying to convey. Positive relationships with local media can save you time, money, and energy. I am not advocating that you should not go out into the community, but I am advocating working smarter not harder. Every successful program attained success by working diligently to accomplish the mission at hand.

The media can be an important asset towards sharing your message with the community; however, they can also have biases too. For example, if your community has not been as transparent as it should have been, and each time information is requested, the media has to go through an act of Congress to get it, you just might have a problem. The solution to this potential problem and problems similar to this one is to be open from the very beginning. Share the data and the reasons why the program will be a good fit for the community. Be forthcoming about the projected cost of the program and stress the need for community support.

Notes

Set A Date For The Grand Opening

Setting a date for the grand opening of your program is sure to be an exciting time, and I know you are looking forward to everything working out as planned. I understand that it is very seldom that things work out like they are supposed to, but that should not stop you from trying to reach that goal. You should take a few things into consideration before confirming your date for the opening.

First, you should confirm the attendance of key community leaders and stakeholders. Those who have contributed will want to have the opportunity to see what impact their investment has made. Regardless of whether or not your city has provided funding for your program, you should ensure that someone from the city is present.

Secondly, you should have the opening at a time when the youth of your community can be present to tour the facility, because after all it is for them. Thirdly, it is important for you to check to see if there are other events held at the same time as your event that might conflict with the grand opening. You should also consider the weather forecast when making your plans. You want the turnout to be as large as possible and inclement weather can put a damper on the opening. However, no one on earth can control the weather, so be prepared to Change your plans, if bad weather is imminent.

Having food at a grand opening is high on the priority list because people like to eat. Food helps fill the void in more ways than one. People often meet and greet each other, while they are eating. There are also times when people come to an event and they are hungry, and because of that, they may not pay close attention to the message or messenger. I am not advocating that you prepare a full buffet, but prepare something.

Notes

Notes

Starting The First Class Of The Youth Program

Congratulations, you and your staff should be very proud of what you have accomplished thus far. Your perseverance and dedication has culminated in the beginning of what will be a new outlook in the lives of the youth of your community. Cherish this moment, and be proud of your accomplishments.

Ensure that you do a few housekeeping activities during your first class meeting. You should introduce yourself and the staff to all the youth participants and ask them to do the same. It would be a good idea to briefly outline the program, and expectations of all the participants. Also, make every effort to get as much data as you can from each child by using your program registration forms, which should include spaces for the name, address, phone number, parent/guardian's name, email address, medical issues, height, weight, hair color, and eye color. It would also be a great idea to have the participants draw a map from your facility to their home.

You'll want to make everyone feel very welcome to the program, if not, they won't come back. There is nothing more disheartening than to have put so much effort into something and no one shows up. Incorporate some fun activities the very first meeting. Your attitude and the attitudes of your staff can be read in a split second. Even though you will be talking about serious issues, you should always try and find a way to impart the information in a kid-friendly manner. I encourage you to have a great time while making positive changes in the lives of young people and your community.

Best Wishes!

Notes

Sample Program Curriculum

There are hundreds and perhaps thousands of different types of curriculum that you may choose to use for your youth program. You may even decide to create your own, and that is a great idea. I have provided a copy of the curriculum that was used in our Mayor's Youth Leadership Institute Program. We tailored this curriculum to fit our community, but you may have a totally different vision and mission in mind. Our goal was to cover a variety of different critical issues that our youth was facing at that time and are still facing today. If you find it helpful to use our guide, then please do not hesitate to do so.

The Mayor's Youth Leadership Institute Curriculum

"We Are Producing World-Class Leaders"

Youth Coordinator: Lynette Mollay

Institute Founded & Curriculum Created By: Mayor Carl Camon, Ed.S

Copyright 2004

Program Introduction

Carl L. Camon, Mayor of Ray City, founded the Mayor's Youth Leadership Institute (MYLI) of Ray City, in 2000. The program's main focus is to ensure that the youth are aware of a variety of factors that influence both positive and negative behaviors, within their respective communities. The MYLI program has made a great impact within the City of Ray City, and a noticeable impact on the youth who have been a part of the program at one point or the other during its ten-year existence.

Program Description

The MYLI conducts a free, two-week intensive training program during the second and third week of July, and during scheduled meetings throughout the year. Youth between the ages of 10 – 17 are encouraged to participate, and there is no class size limit. During the two-weeks we provide snacks, and discuss, in detail, the following important issues:

1. Local, State, & Federal Government (Terms of office, Elections, Voting, Offices held, and by whom; current Governmental Affairs, ex. What's in the news? Branches of Government, etc.), City History and Community Involvement
2. Leadership responsibilities such as: the importance of being your own leader, and the importance of following the right people; Leadership skills scenarios, Qualities of a good leader, ex. Responsible, A Good Listener, Trustworthy, Organized, Understanding, Integrity, Perseverance, etc.
3. Critical Issues Session: Drug, Tobacco, & Alcohol Prevention, Abstinence & Teen Pregnancy Prevention, School Dropout Prevention, Career Choices, Law Enforcement Awareness, & Violence Prevention and Gang Related Issues (just to name a few)

City Life Scenarios

During this session of the training, youth leadership members have an opportunity to literally take control of every day city activities. They become mayors, council members, police & fire chiefs, water & sewer personnel, city clerks, and ordinary adult citizens. We have experienced great success with these real life exercises. Youth comments upon completion of these activities indicated, "they now understand what it is like to be in control of a city".

Life Skills

We have had so much fun teaching this session to our youth. They have the opportunity to cook their own snacks under the supervision of an adult member of our program, and they learn how to iron, fold clothes, sweep a floor, wash clothes, brush their teeth properly, apply deodorant, etc. We feel that personal cleanliness and organization skills are an important part of being a leader.

10 & 25 City Tours

MYLI members had the opportunity to travel by chartered bus, to ten cities one summer and to twenty-five cities, the next summer, to explore and see first hand how the various cities handle their day-to-day operations. This trip was not announced until a day or two before the trip, because the idea was to see a city doing what it usually does without any significant planning for our arrival.

Graduation Ceremony

A graduation ceremony is held each year, and each member who completes the thirty-hour training receives a certificate stating that they have met the requirements of the program. A graduation luncheon is provided at the end of the program.

Summer Educational & Empowerment Trip

The MYLI sponsors an end of training summer trip, as our way of encouraging our youth to stay involved in the community and the program. We have visited places such as: Wild Adventures Theme Park in Valdosta, City Hall in Atlanta, GA, The Chattanooga Aquarium, and a cave and camping in Chattanooga and Collegedale, TN, Montgomery & Selma Alabama to the National Voter's Rights Museum, Atlanta – Carter Center and Museum, the King Center, APEX Museum, World of Coke, and the State Capitol. We have also been invited to participate as a guest of the National Leagues of Cities, Washington, D.C., to various locations around the country to share our program.

Week II

"Guest Speakers Week"

Day Six - <u>Career Planning</u> – Educational Institutions, Teacher, Professors, Department of Labor & Various Businesses

_____

_____

_____

_____

_____

Day Seven – <u>Elected Officials Day</u> – Council Members, Mayors, County Commissioners, Sheriffs, District Attorneys, Judges, State Representatives, State Senators

_____

_____

_____

_____

Day Eight – <u>Prevention Services</u> - Health Department, Social Services, Teen Pregnancy, Sexually Transmitted Diseases (STDs), Drugs, Alcohol, & Cigarette

_____

_____

_____

_____

Day Nine - <u>The Military</u> & Their Role In Our Society

_____

_____

_____

_____

Day Ten - Course Completion Ceremony 1:00 P.M. - Guest Speaker TBA

_____

_____

_____

_____

Chapter One

Ray City History & Community Involvement

The opportunity to embark on a journey to learn as much as you can about the community in which you live should be taken very seriously. One writer said that if a person does not know anything about their past, then how can they effectively plan their future. Your community has grown over the past few decades, and that growth is due to those who have worked hard to make it what it is today. Many people may look at the things that are not available, rather than enjoying the things that are. Ray City has a rich history, which began almost two miles east of its current location. Many years ago, you probably wouldn't have recognized the city's name as Ray City, because it was called Ray's Mill. Yes, you guessed it; the former location of Ray City before it moved farther west was located at what we all know now, as Ray's Mill Pond.

The City was actually named after a man called Mr. Thomas Ray. Some people confuse the name of our city with the name of another city in Georgia called Raye, Georgia. It seems strange to some to say Ray City, or even stranger to say the City of Ray City. Ray City was incorporated in 1909. (We celebrated our Centennial Celebration (100 years old) in 2009.) Over the years, the number of mayors that citizens elect can really add up. There have been over 18 mayors who have had the opportunity to serve our city. In 2001, Mayor Carl Camon and his staff researched old records and made several phone calls to find pictures of the former mayors. Also in 2001, the city sponsored a ceremony to honor the mayors and their families for their commitment and contributions to Ray City. The first mayor of Ray City was named C.X. Jones. During the special ceremony held in Ray City, we were honored to have a great-great grandson of Mayor C.X. Jones present to receive a framed certificate on the deceased mayor's behalf.

(Mayor Carl L. Camon has just completed his fifth term as Mayor of Ray City.) He encourages everyone, especially the youth to get involved in the community. He often explains that if you pick up a piece of paper, or come to city council meetings, then you are being involved. The future of our city depends on our future leaders, and you are one of them. If the citizens of a city are not involved, it is possible that drug dealers or gang members could take over our city. Also, if one does not become involved, the people that are elected to positions of leadership will not know how you as a citizen feel about important issues. Every issue that is discussed in a city directly or indirectly affects all citizens in one-way or another.

City Hall is the place where the Mayor's, City Council's, City Clerk's, and Chief of Police's offices are located. City council meeting is held there as well. The major business of a city is carried out in this building, which is sometimes known as the headquarters of a city. There are other facilities in a city, such as the Wastewater Treatment Facility, which in our case is known as the Oxidation Pond. All of the city's sewer ends up going into the Oxidation Pond. The city also operates an educational facility. This facility has been in existence since 1996, and Ray City is known as the first municipality in the State of Georgia to operate its own Pre-K Program. The Mayor's Youth Leadership Institute is another program that receives funding from the City of Ray City. Mayor Carl L. Camon founded the program. The program's main goal is to ensure that the youth of Ray City are aware of a number of important issues that will help them become more productive citizens, and positive contributors to our society. Always remember that your community is only as strong as its weakest member. That is why it is so important that we continue to empower each other, so that we may train up a generation of leaders who do not mind getting involved and working hard to ensure that their community survives for generations to come.

Notes

The Mayor's Youth Leadership Institute
Ray City, Georgia

City History & Community Involvement

Test I

Student Name_____ Date_____ Instructor_____

1. The City was originally located at what is now called
_____

2. The name of the City before it was renamed to Ray City was called
_____

3. Ray City received its name from a man whose name was
_____

4. The City of Ray City was incorporated in
_____

5. How many mayors have there been in the City of Ray City since being incorporated? _____
_____

6. _____ was the first mayor of Ray City.
7. _____ is the current mayor of Ray City.
8. List two ways that one can become involved in his/her city.
   A.
   B.
9. What are two things that could happen if there is not enough input from citizens regarding how a city should operate?
   A.
   B.
10. What is the name of the facility where the City Clerk, Mayor, City Council, and Chief of Police offices are usually housed?
_____

11. What purpose does City Hall serve?
_____

12. What is the name of the facility where the entire city sewer goes?
_____.

13. The City of Ray City operates its own educational facility, and it is called the
_____.

14. The City of Ray City has a youth program, and it is called the
_____

15. Why do think the Mayor's Youth Leadership Institute is an important program?
_____

Chapter Two

Local, State, & Federal Government

The Mayor's Youth Leadership Institute believes that government works. The way that government works effectively is through a democratic process; that is, the people must have a voice in determining the way that they want their government to work. In underdeveloped countries, there are those who seek to have a voice to express their views on many different issues of concern. However, in many cases, because of the structure of their government, they don't have that freedom to do so. That is why it is very important that those of us, who live in a democracy, utilize our rights as citizens, by getting involved in our respective communities.

We will examine various types of terminology that is directly related to local, state, and national government. Local government is typically a government operated at the local level, usually within a city or town. Local governments may consist of a mayor, city manager, and council members. There are other names for council members, such as, alderman, commissioners, ward leaders, and councilors. Regardless of the names given to the individuals who are elected to govern a city, they all must follow a guidebook of some sort. The guidebook that many local governments use is one granted by their state, and it is commonly known as a Charter. A city's charter has specific guidelines that a city, its governing body, and citizens are to follow. In most cases, the House of Representatives, and the Senate of a state authorizes and issues a charter to a city.

The City Council also has the power to make laws for its city. The laws may be amended (changed) from time to time. These laws are more commonly known as "ordinances". The governing body of a city or town has the right according to the city charter to make and change laws or ordinances as necessary. Some governing bodies ask for advice from its citizenry before they make drastic changes. The number of City Council Members may vary from city to city, mostly depending on the city's size and needs for representation. For example, if you have a city with a population of a thousand people, you may not have a great need for many council members, such as in the case of our city.

Ray City has four council members who are elected to serve for a four-year period of time. Council members are appointed to serve as chairmen/chairwomen over certain departments by the chief executive officer of the city, which is usually the mayor. Many cities have decided to give that same authority to a city manager, or to another appropriate individual. Council members who serve in Ray City are appointed to serve either on the Water & Sewer, Streets & Sanitation, Police & Fire, or Finance Department. As chairman, they provide important information to the mayor, and to the staff assigned to that department. Council members may also co-chair a department. Council members and the mayor may seek re-election to an office as many times as they would like to, because there are no term limits in Ray City. A term limit is the amount of terms that an elected official may serve in a particular elected position.

The state government operates in a similar fashion as the local government, but it receives its charter from the federal (national) government. The state also has guidelines in which it must follow. These guidelines, in many cases are known as articles, which are found within the State's Constitution. The Governor, the chief executive officer of a state, must ensure to the best of his or her ability that the constitution is adhered to. The Lieutenant Governor, which is the assistant governor, must also take a sworn oath to uphold the constitution of the state. The Governor and the Lieutenant Governor hold the two highest offices in the state, and together, they must work to ensure that our state progresses and remains in good condition for future generations.

The Secretary of State has a tremendous responsibility in making sure that the many departments within the state operate at efficient levels as well. There is no way that the Secretary of State can keep up with all that needs to be done in a state by his or herself. Therefore, various commissioners are elected to oversee different departments within the state, and the governor also has the responsibility of appointing some of the individuals to serve as commissioners as well. The state government is similar to the local government, but in most cases, it is much, much larger and more complex.

However, the complexity of the state government does not compare to the enormous complex issues of our federal government. Our federal government is made up of three branches, which are the Executive Branch, Legislative Branch, and the Judicial Branch. Each of the three branches has its own significance, as it relates to the operation of the overall federal government. The Executive Branch is made up of the President and his cabinet members, and their duty is to enforce the laws. The president is the Commander and Chief of a country. Our current President is President Barack Obama, and his cabinet is made up of members that have been selected to serve as "Secretaries" over various departments, such as the Secretary of Defense, and Secretary of Labor. Our Vice-President is Vice-President Joseph Biden. He is the second in command of our country, which is the United States of America.

The Legislative Branch of government is made up of the United States Congress (House of Representatives), and the United States Senate. The Legislative Branch's responsibility is to make the laws that we must follow. Each state is authorized to have two senators who are elected from their state, to represent them in Washington D.C., which is our nation's capitol. The population of that state determines the number of Congressmen, who will go to Washington, to represent any given state. For example, the more people a state has, the more Congressmen that may be elected, and able to represent that state in Washington.

The third branch of government is the called the Judicial Branch, and its primary responsibility is to interpret the laws. The U.S. Supreme Court is the highest court in the United States. It is made up of nine Supreme Court Justices, who are appointed by the President of the United States. The Supreme Court will decide the final decision of a court case, which cannot be resolved in lower-courts. Supreme Court Justices are appointed to serve for life. Therefore they don't have to be elected, and they do not have term limits.

We are hopeful that you will become more interested in the way government works. You are a citizen, and you have that right to know. However, it is up to you to decide how much you want to know about your government. Each level of government desires input from citizens regarding issues that are important to the operation of that particular government. The future of our government, and the way it is operated depends on you. Please remember that all decisions, great and small may have an impact on your life in one way or another. It behooves us all to get involved and stay involved, if we want to continue to see our government remain strong, and vibrant. The democratic process (of the people, by the people, for the people) should not be taken for granted, for there are many who wish that they lived in a free country like ours.

Notes

_____

_____

_____

_____

_____

_____

_____

_____

_____

_____

_____

_____

_____

_____

_____

_____

_____

_____

_____

_____

_____

_____

_____

Notes

The Mayor's Youth Leadership Institute
Ray City, Georgia

Test II

Local, State, & Federal Government

Student Name_____ Date_____ Instructor_____

1. What is a city charter? _____

_____

_____

2. The _____ ___ _____, and the _____,
   passes legislation to issue a city its charter.

3. The _____ _____ is the governing body that has the power to make laws
   for local government.

4. These laws are most commonly known as City

_____

5. Ray City has _____ City Council Members.

6. Name the four city departments of the City of Ray City. _____,
   _____,   _____,
   _____

7. List three names, which may be given to those who serve on the city council.

   A.

   B.

   C.

8. The _____ is the chief executive officer of Ray City.

9. **T** or **F** A City may chose to have a Mayor/City Council form of government or a City
   Manager/City Council form of government.

10. The State _____ is a document, which contains articles and
    amendments that all citizens must follow, and it gives us information on how the state
    should be operated.

11. Who is the chief executive officer of the State of Georgia?

_____

_____

12. The Honorable. _____ _____ serves as Georgia's Lieutenant
    Governor.

13. Who is the Secretary of State of the State of Georgia?

_____

_____

14. Officials that are elected to offices such as the Department of Labor, Department of Agriculture, and appointed by the Governor to the Department of Natural Resources, the Department of Community Affairs, and the Department of Corrections are called

_____

_____.

15. The three branches of our National Government are. _____

_____,

_____, _____

16. _____ _____ is the President of the United States of America.

17. _____ _____ is the Vice-President of the United States of America.

18. What two bodies make up the Legislative Branch of Government? The U.S. _____ _____ _____, and the U.S. _____

19. The _____ _____is the highest level of the Judicial Branch of Government.

20. The officials who are appointed by the President to serve as heads of the U.S. Department of Labor, Department of the Interior, Department of Defense, and the Department of Homeland Security are called _____.

Chapter Three

Voting & Elections

The right to choose is a simple but powerful right that we should all be honored to have. Just imagine sitting down at a restaurant to order your evening meal, and just as you have finished selecting what you want, the waiter says, "Sir or Ma'am, I'm sorry, but I'll have to choose for you." You would probably be outraged. Why? Because you live in a free country, and you have the right to choose whatever it is that you want to eat for dinner. Now, try to imagine living in a country where citizens don't have the right to vote. Yes, there are actually countries where all of the decisions are made by a small group of people. In some countries, one person makes all of the decisions. Today's session focuses on elections, registering to vote and voting.

In the United States, every legal citizen, who is a registered voter, is allowed to vote. Voting is simply making a choice as to which individual or cause you support. Most decisions in our country are made through the process of voting. The people actually have the opportunity to decide how they want things to go. In order to legally vote in Georgia, you have to be at least 18 years old. A person may register to vote at age 17, but may not vote until their 18th birthday (read the back of the voter registration form for more information).

A person may vote on an issue, or for a candidate. Issues may range from whether or not 15-year olds are authorized to get their "learner's permit"; whether or not a person's license may be reinstated after having been found guilty of a DUI (Driving Under The Influence); or whether the government should continue to pay for medicine for senior citizens. These issues are just a few, out of the thousands of issues that are voted on each year. We also go to the polls (a place where an election is held and where a person votes) to elect a candidate. A candidate is someone who has qualified and who seeks to hold an official office. Many candidates establish campaign committees, which are individuals who are organized, and work to help elect the candidate. These committees work hard, sometimes going from door to door asking for support for their candidate.

Regardless of how much a candidate or a committee campaigns, it is up to the registered voters to elect a person to hold an office. The registered voters are individuals who have completed the necessary paperwork, and have the right to vote in an election, which are government organized events specifically designed to elect a candidate. There are other guidelines that voters must follow in order to have the opportunity to vote. Voters have the right to vote in private, and do not have to tell anyone how they voted on a particular issue, or which candidate they selected.

In session two, Local, State, and Federal Government, we briefly discussed term limits. In some cities, and governments, voters have decided to limit the number of terms a person may serve in a particular elected position. For example, the president of the United States is elected to serve for four years and may only serve two four-year terms, which is a total of eight years. However, President Franklin Roosevelt served in excess of three full terms. Search your history books or the Internet to found out exactly how many years he served, and why the people wanted him to serve even more.

Term limits do not apply to all elected positions. The position of Mayor of Ray City does not have a term limit, nor does any of the council members of Ray City. However, the length of time that they are elected to serve is for four-years at a time. The State and U.S. House of Representative members may serve for two years at a time. In most cases, they are not bound by term limits. A United States Senator's term is six years, and in most cases they are not bound by term limits either. Once a U.S. Supreme Court Justice is appointed, and confirmed by the U.S. Legislature, they can serve for life.

During every national election, which is usually held in November, many people look forward to the opportunity to vote. It is indeed an honor to have right to vote. That is why it is important not to do anything that could take that right away. If a person commits a crime, which is deemed as a felony, that person will most likely lose their right to vote. That may not seem like it is serious, but it is. That simply means that you will not have the right to choose who will represent you in anything. For example, if a decision is considered that would reduce the retirement age to 60, or to give you 75% of the taxes that you paid in, back, and someone votes against doing that; then you will understand how important it is to maintain the right to vote, because that decision directly affects your well-being.

We want everyone to become actively involved, and register to vote as soon as you are of age. It is also important to encourage all of your friends to register and to vote, so that their voices can be heard, as well. They may not currently understand the positive impact that their vote will have, but they will realize it later. Trust me! The future of our city, state and country depends on the decisions that we make, by exercising our right to vote. Remember to vote in every election.

Notes

Notes

The Mayor's Youth Leadership Institute
Ray City, Georgia

Test III

Voting & Elections

Student **Name**_____ **Date**_____ **Instructor**_____

1. What is the legal age that a person can register to vote in Georgia?
_____

2. What is the legal age that a person can vote in Georgia?
_____

3. A _____ is the name that is given to an individual who has applied/qualified for, and seeks to hold a public office.

4. A _____ _____ is an individual who exercises his/her right to select the person of their choice through the election process, to hold an official public office.

5. A _____ is a type of organized movement or crusade that is conducted by a person or a committee representing a person seeking to be elected to hold an office.

6. A _____ _____ signifies the number of times that a person may be elected to serve in a particular elected position.

7. How many terms may the President of the United States serve?
_____

8. How many terms may the Mayor of Ray City serve?
_____

9. An _____ is an officially organized event authorized by a government whereby individuals (citizens) who are registered to vote, may vote to select the candidate of their choice.

10. What is the term of service for someone elected to hold an office in Ray City?_____
_____

11.

12. The election of a governor or a president comes around every _____ years.

13. The election of a U.S. Congressman comes around every _____ years.

14. The election of a U.S. Senator comes around every ____ years.

15. A Supreme Court Justice is appointed for what length of time?
_____

16. T or F A person with a felony will loose his/her right to vote.
17. National elections are usually held during the month of

_____

_____

.

18. Why is it important to register to vote? _____

_____

_____

19. Why is it important to vote?

_____

_____

Notes

Notes

The Mayor's Youth Leadership Institute
Ray City, Georgia

Chapter Four

A Focus On Education

Education can simply be defined as the process of learning. Our society encourages us to obtain as much knowledge as we can. Knowledge is indeed power. The answers to many of our questions may be found by simply learning all that we can learn about a certain situation or topic. The Mayor's Youth Leadership Institute has included an educational component into its curriculum just to briefly inform its members about the process that our society uses to educate its citizens. Our brief awareness session does not even scratch the surface, regarding all of the information that is available to our members and participants.

One important aspect of education that we all should be aware of is that many states require children to begin school by the age of 6 years old. Those parents or guardians who do not obey the law may be taken to court, and forced to put their child in school. However, parents do have the right to teach their children at home. This is known as Home School. Regardless of which style of school that a parent chooses for their child, the important thing to remember is that there are benefits of attending some type of school. A good education can mean the difference between a good job, a nice home, and money in the bank; and having a bad job, no home, and no money in the bank.

Even though most of our members have completed Primary School, which is usually Pre-K through Second Grade, some may not understand that Primary School is normally the first level in the Public School educational process. Yes, most of them already know that they attended primary school, but they know nothing about it being a level within a process. Elementary School (3rd-5th grade), Middle School (6th –8th grade), and High School (9th-12th grade), are the other levels in the Public School process. All of these levels, although similar, are designed to meet different criteria, and accomplish different goals. Also, from state to state, the levels above may be listed in different categories.

It is important that we treat each level with the respect that it deserves. As stated earlier, each grade has its own significance, and if a student cannot or does not recognize it, they will more than likely begin to lag behind. When this occurs, some students may feel that they don't belong in school, therefore many will become dropouts; in other words, they will not complete their education.

Having proper studying habits is an effective tool toward learning, as well as getting good grades on an assignment or test. Some students feel that it is not necessary to study because they already know the material on the test. Research has proven that the more often you study, the longer the information will remain with you. For example, your science teacher presents a 3-day lecture on photosynthesis, and she asks you to remember several important points, and you go home and study each night, you will more than likely be more prepared for the test than someone who waits until the last minute to study. Therefore, good study habits and completing your homework, both give you the opportunity to be successful in school.

A determinant of your success is tested at different levels. There are tests given to students in all levels of public and private school systems. When a student completes the requirements of high school, and passes all the required evaluations and tests; he or she will receive a diploma, which indicates that they have completed a certain level of education. A person must have a high school diploma or a GED in order to be accepted to serve in the military or most post secondary educational institutions. A student who has a desire to continue their education at a technical school, college, or university may be required to take the Scholastic Aptitude Test (SAT). The SAT is a test that helps determine a student's Scholastic Aptitude (the level of knowledge learned in school).

Once a student has decided to further his or her education at an institution of higher learning, they can work toward earning a degree. A degree is similar to a diploma, but there are many variations of degrees that one may receive. We will briefly discuss three of the many degree categories. The first degree is an Associate's Degree, and it is bestowed to an individual who completes a two-year course of study, normally at a Junior College. The second type of degree is a Bachelor's Degree, and this is bestowed to a person who completes a four-year course of study at a college or university. The third type of degree is the Master's Degree, which is awarded when a student successfully completes a five to six year course of study at a college or university. The length of time, and courses of study may vary depending on the student and the requirements of the degree and school.

Some people may decide not to further their education at an institution of higher learning, but may instead decide to get a job that doesn't require a degree. Whatever choice you decide to make is up to you. However, you should remember that a good education might make the difference between making $15,000.00 a year, and $50,000.00 a year. Also, having the satisfaction of knowing that no one can take away the knowledge that you have obtained, will give you a sense of accomplishment. Stay in School, and get a good Education.

Notes

The Mayor's Youth Leadership Institute
Ray City, Georgia

Test Four

A Focus On Education

1. _____ may simply be defined as the process of learning.

2. More knowledge, a good job and salary, a nice home, and personal satisfaction are some of the _____ of getting a good education.

3. In most states, it is a law that children must start school by age _____.

4. Proper _____ _____ usually results in getting good grades on an assignment or test.

5. _____ is important because it gives you an opportunity to review over information learned at school that day, prepares you for new information, and to be successful.

6. In most public schools, Pre-Kindergarten through Second Grade is known as _____ _____ School.

7. In most public schools, Third Grade through Fifth Grade is known as _____ School.

8. In most public schools, Sixth Grade through Eighth Grade is known as _____ School.

9. In most public schools, Ninth Grade through Twelfth Grade is known as _____ School.

10. Most branches of the military, and colleges, and universities, require you to have a high school _____ or GED in order to enlist or enroll.

11. A student in a public/private school system who, decides not to complete their education is commonly know as a

    _____ _____.

12. The successful completion of end of course _____ and/or _____ is required, in order to receive a diploma from most high schools.

13. The _____ _____ _____ is one of the test given to those students who plan to continue their education at the college or university level.

14. List three types of schools a student may attend once they have graduated from high school.

    A.

    B.

C.

15. List the types of degrees that one may obtain according to the years of education that they receive.

    A. 2 years _____

    B. 4 years _____

    C. 5 to 6 years _____

16. List two reasons why it is important to get a good education.

    A.

    B.

Notes

The Mayor's Youth Leadership Institute
Ray City, Georgia

Chapter Five

Developing Leadership Skills

Leadership is the ability to guide and direct others. In every aspect of life, you are most likely to find someone in a leadership position. Whether they are serving as an elected official, a chief of police, a principal, a teacher, a pastor, or even as a part of a community club. Positions of leadership should be taken very seriously. Each day of our lives we should strive to become better leaders. Everyone, at one time or another has probably held some type of leadership position. Your position of leadership could have been when you led the rest of your class in a straight line to the water fountain or to the lunchroom.

We are taught to follow the examples of others. When we are at home, we follow our parents, and when we are in school, we follow our teachers. Regardless of where we are, we have followed someone at one time or another. In order to become a good leader, one must first learn to be a good follower. As a follower, you have the opportunity to notice all of the skills exhibited by the one you are following. If that person is a good leader, you will be able to trust him/her, and he or she will be honest and dependable.

Some leaders procrastinate, but good leaders always plan ahead of time. It is important to always have a plan. There are situations that you may not be able to control, but plan effectively to control the ones you can, especially when there are others who depend on your leadership. It is common for some to say, "If he/she would have just listened to our suggestions, we wouldn't be having the problem that we're having". A statement like the one above is very true, because good leaders focus and listen to good advice, before a decision is made.

Some people are given opportunities to hold leadership positions, but are not good leaders for one reason or the other. Others are trained to become leaders, and further develop those skills over time. There are those who are said to be "born to lead", thus the term, 'born leader". These born leaders may have inborn traits of leadership or they may have had past experiences that have enabled them to become effective leaders. Good leaders also know that it is okay to ask others for help, if the need arises.

There are occasions when leaders have to play multiple roles. If a situation gets to the point where everyone is upset, angry, and at war with each other, the leader has to play the role of a peacemaker. Our jobs, families, and other happenings in our lives may become stressful at times, and one might say something or respond in a way that might be misunderstood by another person. A good leader is skilled at diffusing complicated matters, and doing what is best for all parties involved.

We will know that we are on the path to becoming good leaders, when we learn to respect those in leadership positions. Everyone makes mistakes from time to time, so we must remember that we all are human, and we shouldn't belittle anyone who has made a mistake. Also, good leaders will admit their mistakes, and strive to become better at whatever it is they are doing. A good leader never looks down, in a negative way at anyone, but instead encourages others to succeed and be the very best that they can be.

Men and women, girls and boys can be leaders. A person just needs to have a desire to lead, and work hard toward developing their own style of leadership, because no two people lead in quite the same way. That is why organizations go through great strides in their search for good leaders. Companies often look for individuals with some degree of formal education to hold leadership positions.

There are leaders who have the ability to compel others to follow them. They are very charismatic and fascinating. Sometimes just their smile and the way they talk captivates a person or group of people. Regardless if you are a Born Leader, Trained Leader, or Charismatic Leader, it is important that you remember to take care of those who are under your leadership. Because the skills that they learn from you, will more than likely be passed on to those who will someday follow them. So, remember that your examples of leadership, whether good or bad, will be passed on to someone else. Be good followers, and good leaders. Most of all do what is right.

Notes

The Mayor's Youth Leadership Institute
Ray City, Georgia

Test V

Developing Leadership Skills

1. _____ is the ability to guide and direct others to accomplish a given task.

2. One must become a good _____, before he or she can effectively lead others.

3. A good leader must be _____, _____, and _____.

4. Some leaders may procrastinate, but good leaders _____ ahead of time.

5. If a person is not a good _____, then it will be difficult for that person to hear and understand what the mission is.

6. T or F Everyone that is put in a leadership position, automatically becomes successful at leading others.

7. A good leader analyzes the problem, then asks others for

_____.

8. When situations are out of control and everyone involved is angry and upset, and at war with each other, a good leader should play the role of a _____.

9. T or F There are "Born Leaders", and there are "Trained Leaders"

10. List two reasons why you think it is important to respect those who are in leadership positions.

    A.

    B.

11. Tell us of one situation in which you emerged as the leader.

12. A _____ leader is somewhat charming, captivating, and fascinating, and has the ability to attract others into following him.

13. T or F Men and Women, Girls and Boys can be in leadership positions.

14. People who seek leadership positions will more than likely be required to have some degree of formal _____.

15. Are you a good leader? Explain.

_____

_____

_____

Attendance & Grade Summary

Week I	Present	Absent	Verifying Signature
Day I	_____	_____	_____
Day II	_____	_____	_____
Day III	_____	_____	_____
Day IV	_____	_____	_____
Day V	_____	_____	_____

Week II	Present	Absent	Verifying Signature
Day VI	_____	_____	_____
Day VII	_____	_____	_____
Day VIII	_____	_____	_____
Day IX	_____	_____	_____
Day X	_____	_____	_____

Test Grades

Test I _____

Test II _____

Test III _____

Test IV _____

Test V _____

Behavior Grades

Day - 1	2	3	4	5
——	——	——	——	——

Day - 6	7	8	9	10
——	——	——	——	——

Total Course Score _____

_____ Student Successfully Completed Coursework

_____ Student Did Not Successfully Complete Coursework

_____   _____
Authorized Signature   Date

City Life Scenarios

I have also included a copy of what I call "City Life Scenarios". These were actual scenarios that were played out during our program. I remember the excitement on the faces of our youth when they had the opportunity to take on the role of mayor, city clerk, police chief, fireman, and public works superintendent. We informed the media that we were going to carry out these activities and they gladly covered the story, which was a huge success.

City Life Scenarios Activities

The goal of the City Life scenarios is to increase the awareness of the everyday operations of a city. We accomplished this goal by having the youth leadership members experience what it was like to work for a local municipal government. Each participant assumed the role of a city employee or city official, and performed their respective assigned duties. There are seven scenarios that make up the City Life exercise.

<u>Scenario I</u> - City Clerk & Assistant City Clerk

Youth leadership members will assume the role of the City Clerk and Acting City Clerk. The City Clerk will be tasked to count money in order to make a bank deposit. They will be required to write down the amount that they counted and the real City Clerk will recount the money, but will remove some of the money to make the amount different, and return the money to the acting City Clerk to recount. Once the money is recounted, it will be once again returned to the real City Clerk and the money that was taken out will be added back in again. The real City Clerk must not allow the acting City Clerk to see the money when it is removed or returned. Continue this at least twice.

The acting City Clerk will receive several phone calls, while the real City Clerk is counting the money. Angry citizens will be calling in and complaining, and the acting City Clerk will be required to fill out the city complaint forms.

While the real City Clerk is counting the money, and the acting City Clerk is filling out complaint forms, someone will call in on the radio to give a water meter reading to the acting City Clerk. While the acting City Clerk is taking down the water meter reading, the phone will ring and the governor (someone pretending to be the governor) will be on the line, and he will ask to speak to the mayor.

Scenario II - The Mayor

The Governor has received information that someone is breaking the law by not adhering to the State Water Restrictions posted by the Environmental Protection Department (EPD). He is really upset and is thinking about coming down to talk to the Mayor personally.
Scenario II continues…

As soon as the Mayor is finished talking with the Governor, and hangs up the phone, an angry citizen walks through the door complaining about the trash on Main St., in front of City Hall. The angry citizen asks the Mayor to come outside and take a look at the trash. When the Mayor comes outside, he will notice a pile of trash that has been dumped in front of City Hall. The citizen will continue to be upset and tell the Mayor that the people are going to vote him out of office if he doesn't clean up this town.

Scenario III – The City Workers Streets Department

The real Superintendent walks up with the acting Superintendent and tells him to ask what is going on. The angry citizen gets upset with both the Mayor, and the Superintendent.   The Superintendent will instruct the little city workers (younger youth members) to pick up the trash in front of city hall.
While the Mayor is outside someone will call on the radio and tell the acting City Clerk to tell the Police Chief that a prisoner escaped from the prison in Valdosta, GA, and stole a car and is headed toward Ray City.

Scenario IV– The Police Chief

The real Chief of Police needs to tell the acting Police Chief to tell the Mayor that an escaped prisoner is headed toward Ray City. When the acting Police Chief tells the Mayor; the real Chief of Police will ask him why is he telling the Mayor? (Put the pressure on the acting Police Chief.) Cause a disturbance for about two to three minutes, while giving a call sign to a participating sheriff's deputy (involve as many agencies as you can) to stage an accident just out of the way of the intersection in the middle of town, involving the escaped convict and an innocent driver in another car.
Then the acting Police Chief will get a call about an accident in Ray City at the intersection. The acting Police Chief will get into the car with the real Police Chief and they will ride down to the accident scene. The real Police Chief will ask if the acting Police Chief has called the ambulance, if not, tell him to call the ambulance. The ambulance needs to be out of site until it is called, and then it will come with the full siren and the lights. The real Police Chief will tell the acting Police Chief to explain to the paramedics what happened. As soon as the ambulance is there for about five minutes, someone will call the Water & Sewer Superintendent on the radio about a broken main water line in the Beaver Subdivision

Scenario V– The Water Department (Superintendent)

The real Superintendent will encourage the acting Superintendent to get into the truck with him, so that they can go and repair the water line. The real Superintendent should allow the acting Superintendent to get his or her hands dirty, while helping to repair the busted water line. Wait about five or so minutes until the repairs on the line is almost complete. Then the City clerk will get a call about a fire at the Ray City Pre-K on Pauline St.

Scenario VI – The Acting Firefighters & The Fire Department

Someone will pull the fire whistle at the fire station, and the firefighters will suit up in their suits. The acting firefighter will ride with the real firefighters to the location of the fire. The real firefighter will allow the acting firefighter to give the directions to the fire. Just tell them that it is at the Pre-K, but let the firefighter tell you where to drive. Do a demonstration with the hoses and spray some water near the playground, when finished with the fire demonstration (about 5 – 10 minutes), we will end the exercise, and return to the Youth Center, to discuss the events of the day.

The people who held these actual positions will have the opportunity to explain in more detail about what their jobs entailed. When the discussion is over, the City Life Exercise will end.

50 State Resource Guide

There are thousands of different types of resources available to you and your program. Provided below is a list of state agencies from all fifty states and the District of Columbia. These agencies may be able to provide you with some valuable information about substance abuse, mental health issues, drugs and alcohol use prevention and other social services. I encourage you to log on to the website of the agency from your state and ask them to send you a packet of information associated with the issues that concern you and your community the most.

ALABAMA
Substance Abuse Services Division
Alabama Department of Mental Health and Mental Retardation
RSA Union Building
100 North Union Street
Montgomery, Alabama 36130-1410
TELEPHONE: (334) 242-3953
FACSIMILE: (334) 242-0759
URL http://www.mh.alabama.gov/SA/index.htm

ALASKA
Division of Behavioral Health
Alaska Department of Health and Social Services
3601 C Street, Suite 934
Anchorage, Alaska 99503
TELEPHONE: (907) 269-3410
FACSIMILE: (907) 465-5864
URL http://www.hss.state.ak.us/dbh/

ARIZONA
Arizona Department of Health Services
Division of Behavioral Health Services
150 North 18th Avenue, Suite 220
Phoenix, Arizona 85007-3228
TELEPHONE: (602) 364-4626
FACSIMILE: (602) 364.4570
URL http://www.azdhs.gov/bhs/

ARKANSAS
Office of Alcohol and Drug Abuse Prevention
Division of Behavioral Health Services
Arkansas Department of Health and Human Services
4800 W. 7th Street
Little Rock, Arkansas 72205
TELEPHONE: (501) 686-9871
FACSIMILE: (501) 686-9035
URL http://www.arkansas.gov/dhhs/dmhs/

CALIFORNIA
California Department of Alcohol and Drug Programs
1700 K Street, Fifth Floor Executive Office
Sacramento, California 95811-4022
TELEPHONE: (916) 445-1943
FACSIMILE: (916) 324-7338
URL http://www.adp.cahwnet.gov/

COLORADO
Colorado Department of Human Services
3824 West Princeton Circle, Building 15 Denver, Colorado 80236-3111
TELEPHONE: (303) 866-7486
FACSIMILE: (303) 866-7428
URL http://www.cdhs.state.co.us/adad/

CONNECTICUT
Connecticut Department of Mental Health and Addiction Services
P.O. Box 341431
Hartford, Connecticut 06134
TELEPHONE: (860) 418-6700
FACSIMILE: (860) 418-6691
URL http://www.dmhas.state.ct.us/

DELAWARE
Division of Substance Abuse and Mental Health
Delaware Health and Social Services
1901 N. DuPont Highway, Main Building 1st Floor
New Castle, Delaware 19720
TELEPHONE: (302) 255-9404
FACSIMILE: (302) 255-4427
URL http://www.dhss.delaware.gov/dhss/dsamh/index.htm

FLORIDA
Substance Abuse Program Office
Florida Department of Children and Families
1317 Winewood Boulevard, Building 6, Room 300
Tallahassee, Florida 32399-0700
TELEPHONE: (850) 921-2495
FACSIMILE: (850) 487-2627
URL http://www.state.fl.us/cf_web/

GEORGIA
Division of Addictive Diseases
Georgia Department of Behavioral Health and Developmental Disabilities
2 Peachtree Street, N.W. , Suite 22-273 Atlanta, Georgia 30303-3171 TELEPHONE: (404) 657-2331
FACSIMILE: (404) 657-2256
URL http://mhddad.dhr.georgia.gov/portal/site/DBHDD/

HAWAII
Alcohol and Drug Abuse Division
Behavioral Health Administration
Hawaii State Department of Health
Kakuhihewa Building
601 Kamokila Boulevard, Room 360
Kapolei, Hawaii 96707
TELEPHONE: (808) 692-7506
FACSIMILE: (808) 692-7521
URL http://www.hawaii.gov/health/substance-abuse/

IDAHO
Division of Behavioral Health
Idaho Department of Health and Welfare
450 West State Street, 3rd Floor
P. O. Box 83720
Boise, Idaho 83720-0036
TELEPHONE: (208) 334-5756
FACSIMILE: (208) 332-7305
URL http://www.healthandwelfare.idaho.gov/

ILLINOIS
Illinois Department of Human Services
Division of Alcoholism and Substance Abuse
James R. Thompson Center
100 West Randolph Street, Suite 5-600
Chicago, Illinois 60601
TELEPHONE: (312) 814-2300
FACSIMILE: (312) 814-2419
URL http://www.dhs.state.il.us/oasa/

INDIANA
Office of Addiction and Emergency Preparedness
Division of Mental Health and Addiction
Indiana Family and Social Services Administration
402 W. Washington Street
Indiana Government Building, Room W353
Indianapolis, Indiana 46204-2739
TELEPHONE: (317) 232-7913
FACSIMILE: (317) 233-3472
URL http://www.in.gov/fssa/mental/addiction.html

IOWA
Division of Behavioral Health and Professional Licensure
Iowa Department of Public Health
321 East 12th Street
Lucas State Office Building, 4th Floor
Des Moines, Iowa 50319-0075
TELEPHONE: (515) 281-4417
FACSIMILE: (515) 281-4535
URL http://www.idph.state.ia.us/bh/substance_abuse.asp

KANSAS
Addiction and Prevention Services
Department of Social and Rehabilitation Services
915 SW Harrison Street
Topeka, Kansas 66612
TELEPHONE: (785) 296-6807
FACSIMILE: (785) 296-7275
URL http://www.srskansas.org/

KENTUCKY
Division of Behavioral Health
Kentucky Department for Behavioral Health, Developmental, and Intellectual Disabilities
100 Fair Oaks Lane, 4E-D
Frankfort, Kentucky 40621-0001
TELEPHONE: (502) 564-4456
FACSIMILE: (502) 564-9010
URL http://mhmr.ky.gov/mhsas/default.asp?sub2|sub90

LOUISIANA
Office for Addictive Disorders
Louisiana Department of Health and Hospitals
The Bienville Building 628 North 4th Street, 4th Floor
P.O. Box 2790, BIN #18
Baton Rouge, Louisiana 70821-2790
TELEPHONE: (225) 342-6717
FACSIMILE: (225) 342-3875
URL http://www.dhh.state.la.us/offices/?ID=23

MAINE
Office of Substance Abuse
Maine Department of Health and Human Services
41 Anthony Avenue
11 State House Station
Augusta, Maine 04333-0011
TELEPHONE: (207) 287-2595/6330
FACSIMILE: (207) 287-4334
URL http://www.maine.gov/dhhs/osa/

MARYLAND
Alcohol and Drug Abuse Administration
Maryland Department of Health and Mental Hygiene
55 Wade Avenue
Catonsville, Maryland 21228
TELEPHONE: (410) 402-8610
FACSIMILE: (410) 402-8601
URL http://maryland-adaa.org/

MASSACHUSETTS
Bureau of Substance Abuse Services
Massachusetts Department of Public Health
250 Washington Street, 3rd Floor
Boston, Massachusetts 02108-4609
TELEPHONE: (617) 624-5151
FACSIMILE: (617) 624-5185
URL http://www.mass.gov/dph/bsas/bsas.htm

MICHIGAN
Office of Drug Control Policy
Michigan Department of Community Health
Lewis Cass Building, 5th Floor
320 South Walnut Street,
Lansing, Michigan 48913
TELEPHONE: (517) 241-2600
FACSIMILE: (517) 241-2611
URL http://www.michigan.gov/odcp

MINNESOTA
Alcohol and Drug Abuse Division
Minnesota Department of Human Services
P.O. Box 94977
St. Paul, Minnesota 55164-0977
TELEPHONE: (651) 431-2457
FACSIMILE: (651) 431-7449
URL http://www.dhs.state.mn.us

MISSISSIPPI
Division of Alcohol and Drug Abuse
Mississippi Department of Mental Health
1101 Robert E. Lee Building
239 North Lamar Street, Suite 801
Jackson, Mississippi 39201
TELEPHONE: (601) 359-6220
FACSIMILE: (601) 359-6295
URL http://www.dmh.state.ms.us/substance_abuse.htm

MISSOURI
Division of Alcohol and Drug Abuse
Missouri Department of Mental Health
1706 East Elm Street
P.O. Box 687
Jefferson City, Missouri 65102-0687
TELEPHONE: (573) 751-4942
FACSIMILE: (573) 751-7814
URL http://www.dmh.missouri.gov/ada/adaindex.htm

MONTANA
Chemical Dependency Bureau
Addictive and Mental Disorders Division
Montana Department of Public Health and Human Services
P.O. Box 202905
Helena, Montana 59620-2905
TELEPHONE: (406) 444-6981

FACSIMILE: (406) 444-4435
URL http://www.dphhs.mt.gov/amdd/

NEBRASKA
Division of Behavioral Health
Nebraska Department of Health and Human Services
P.O. Box 95026
Nebraska State Office Building
301 Centennial Mall
Lincoln, NE 68509-5026
TELEPHONE: (402) 471-8553
FACSIMILE: (402) 471-9449
URL http://www.hhss.ne.gov/sua/suaindex.htm

NEVADA
Substance Abuse Prevention and Treatment Agency
Division of Mental Health and Developmental Services
Nevada Department of Health and Human Services
4126 Technology Way, 2nd Floor
Carson City, Nevada 89706-2027
TELEPHONE: (775) 684-4190
FACSIMILE: (775) 684-4185
URL http://mhds.state.nv.us/

NEW HAMPSHIRE
Bureau of Drug and Alcohol Services
Division of Community Based Care Services
New Hampshire Department of Health and Human Services
Main Building
105 Pleasant Street, 3rd Floor North
Concord, New Hampshire 03301
TELEPHONE: (603) 271-6105 or 6100
FACSIMILE: (603) 271-6116
URL http://www.dhhs.state.nh.us/DHHS/ATOD/default.htm

NEW JERSEY
Division of Addiction Services
New Jersey Department of Human Services
120 South Stockton Street, 3rd Floor
P.O. Box 362
Trenton, New Jersey 08625-0362
TELEPHONE: (609) 292-5760
FACSIMILE: (609) 292-3816
URL http://www.state.nj.us/humanservices/das/about%20DAS.htm

NEW MEXICO
Behavioral Health Collaborative
New Mexico Human Services Department
37 Plaza La Prensa
Post Office Box 2348
Santa Fe, New Mexico 87507
TELEPHONE: (505) 476-9257
FACSIMILE: (505) -476-9277
URL http://www.bhd.state.nm.us/

NEW YORK
New York State Office of Alcoholism and Substance Abuse Services
1450 Western Avenue
Albany, New York 12203-3526
TELEPHONE: (518) 457-1758
FACSIMILE: (518) 457-5474
URL http://www.oasas.state.ny.us/index.cfm

NORTH CAROLINA
Community Policy Management
Division of Mental Health, Developmental Disabilities and Substance Abuse
North Carolina Department of Health and
Human Services
3007 Mail Service Center
Raleigh, North Carolina 27699-3007
TELEPHONE: (919) 733-4670
FACSIMILE: (919) 733-9455
URL http://www.ncdhhs.gov/mhddsas/

NORTH DAKOTA
Division of Mental Health and Substance
Abuse Services
North Dakota Department of Human Services
Prairie Hills Plaza
1237 West Divide Avenue, Suite 1C
Bismarck, North Dakota 58501-1208
TELEPHONE: (701) 328-8924
FACSIMILE: (701) 328-8969
URL http://www.nd.gov/dhs/services/mentalhealth/

OHIO
Ohio Department of Alcohol and Drug Addiction Services
280 North High Street, 12th Floor
Columbus, Ohio 43215-2537
TELEPHONE: (614) 752-8359 or 466-3445
FACSIMILE: (614) 752-8645

URL http://www.odadas.state.oh.us

OKLAHOMA
Oklahoma Department of Mental Health and
Substance Abuse Services
1200 N.E. 13th Street
P.O. Box 53277
Oklahoma City, Oklahoma 73152-3277
TELEPHONE: (405) 522-3877
FACSIMILE: (405) 522-0637
URL http://www.odmhsas.org/ or http://www.odmhsas.org/subab.htm

OREGON
Addiction and Mental Health Division
Oregon Department of Human Services
500 Summer Street, NE, E-86
Salem, Oregon 97301-1118
TELEPHONE: (503) 945-5922
FACSIMILE: (503) 373-8327
URL http://www.oregon.gov/DHS/addiction/index.shtml

PENNSYLVANIA
Bureau of Drug and Alcohol Programs
Pennsylvania Department of Health
02 Klein Plaza, Suite B
Harrisburg, Pennsylvania 17104
TELEPHONE: (717) 787-2712
FACSIMILE: (717) 787-6285
URL http://www.dsf.health.state.pa.us/health/site/default.asp

RHODE ISLAND
Division of Behavioral Healthcare Services
Rhode Island Department of Mental Health, Retardation and Hospitals
14 Harrington Road-Barry Hall
Cranston, Rhode Island 02920
TELEPHONE: (401) 462-2339
FACSIMILE: (401) 462-6636
URL http://www.mhrh.state.ri.us/SA/

SOUTH CAROLINA
South Carolina Department of Alcohol and Other Drug Abuse Services
101 Executive Center Drive, Suite 215
Columbia, South Carolina 29210
TELEPHONE: (803) 896-5555
FACSIMILE: (803) 896-5557
URL http://www.daodas.state.sc.us/

SOUTH DAKOTA
Division of Alcohol and Drug Abuse
South Dakota Department of Human Services
E Highway 34, Hillsview Properties Plaza
c/o 500 E. Capitol Avenue
Pierre, South Dakota 57501-5070
TELEPHONE: (605) 773-3123/5990
FACSIMILE: (605) 773-7076
URL http://dhs.sd.gov/ada/

TENNESSEE
Tennessee Department of Mental Health and Developmental Disabilities
425 5th Avenue North, 1st Floor
Cordell Hull Building
Nashville, Tennessee 37243
TELEPHONE: (615) 741-1921
FACSIMILE: (615) 532-2419
URL http://www.state.tn.us/mental/index.html
or http://www2.state.tn.us/health/A&D/index.htm

TEXAS
Mental Health and Substance Abuse Division
Texas Department of State Health Services
P.O. Box 149397
Mail Code 2053
Austin, Texas 78714-9347
TELEPHONE: (512) 206-5968
FACSIMILE: (512) 206-5718
URL http://www.dshs.state.tx.us/sa/default.shtm

UTAH
Division of Substance Abuse and Mental Health
Utah Department of Human Services
120 North 200 West, Room 209
Salt Lake City, Utah 84103
TELEPHONE: (801) 538-3939
FACSIMILE: (801) 538-9892
URL http://www.dsamh.utah.gov/

VERMONT
Alcohol and Drug Abuse Programs
Agency of Human Services
Vermont Department of Health
108 Cherry Street
PO Box 70

Burlington, Vermont 05402-0070
TELEPHONE: (802) 951-1258
FACSIMILE: (802) 951-1275
URL http://healthvermont.gov/adap/adap.aspx

VIRGINIA
Office of Substance Abuse Services
Virginia Department of Behavioral Health and Developmental Services
1220 Bank Street, 8th Floor
P.O. Box 1797
Richmond, Virginia 23219-1797
TELEPHONE: (804) 786-3906
FACSIMILE: (804) 371-6638
URL http://www.dmhmrsas.virginia.gov/OSAS-default.htm

WASHINGTON
Division of Alcohol and Substance Abuse
Washington Department of Social and Health Services
P.O. Box 45330
Olympia, Washington 98504-5330
TELEPHONE: (360) 725-3700
FACSIMILE: (360) 438-8078
URL http://www1.dshs.wa.gov/dasa/

WEST VIRGINIA
Division of Alcohol and Drug Abuse
Office of Behavioral Health Services
Bureau for Behavioral Health and Health Facilities
West Virginia Department of Health and Human Services
350 Capitol Street-Room 350
Charleston, West Virginia 25301-3702
TELEPHONE: (304) 558-6480
FACSIMILE: (304) 558-1008
URL http://www.wvdhhr.org/bhhf/ada.asp

WISCONSIN
Division of Mental Health and Substance Abuse Services
Wisconsin Department of Health Services
1 West Wilson Street-Room 434
P.O. Box 7850
Madison, Wisconsin 53707-7850
TELEPHONE: (608) 267-9391
FACSIMILE: (608) 266-1533
URL http://dhs.wisconsin.gov/substabuse/

WYOMING
Mental Health and Substance Abuse Services Division
Wyoming Department of Health
6101 North Yellowstone Road, Suite 220
Cheyenne, Wyoming 82002-0480
TELEPHONE: (307) 777-6494
FACSIMILE: (307) 777-5849
URL http://wdh.state.wy.us/mhsa/index.html

DISTRICT OF COLUMBIA
Addiction Prevention and Recovery Administration
District of Columbia Department of Health
1300 First Street, NE, Suite 319
Washington, DC 20002-3314
TELEPHONE: (202) 727-8941
FACSIMILE: (202) 727-0092
URL http://dchealth.dc.gov/doh

State Municipal Leagues

Below is a complete list of the state municipal leagues that are located in the United States. Each of these leagues can provide you with a wealth of data to help you get your program started. You should make it a practice to attend your league's annual conferences. More times than not, you will have the opportunity to find out what youth programs are already in existence in your state. The State of Hawaii did not have a municipal league as of the date that this guide was published.

ALABAMA LEAGUE OF MUNICIPALITIES
P.O. Box 1270
535 Adams Avenue
Montgomery, Alabama 36102
(334) 262-2566

ALASKA MUNICIPAL LEAGUE
217 Second Street, Suite 200
Juneau, Alaska 99801
(907) 586-1325

LEAGUE OF ARIZONA CITIES AND TOWNS
1820 West Washington Street
Phoenix, Arizona 85007
(602) 258-5786

ARKANSAS MUNICIPAL LEAGUE
P.O. Box 38 (301 W. 2nd Street - 72114)
North Little Rock, Arkansas 72115
(501) 374-3484

LEAGUE OF CALIFORNIA CITIES
1400 K Street, 4th Floor
Sacramento, California 95814
(916) 658-8200

COLORADO MUNICIPAL LEAGUE
1144 Sherman Street
Denver, Colorado 80203
(303) 831-6411

CONNECTICUT CONFERENCE OF MUNICIPALITIES
900 Chapel Street, 9th Floor
New Haven, Connecticut 06510-2807
(203) 498-3000

DELAWARE LEAGUE OF LOCAL GOVERNMENTS
P.O. Box 484 1210 White Oak Road - 19903-0475
Dover, Delaware 9903-0475
(302) 678-0991

FLORIDA LEAGUE OF CITIES
P.O. Box 1757 301 South Bronough,
Suite 300 - 32301
Tallahassee, Florida 32302-1757
(850) 222-9684

GEORGIA MUNICIPAL ASSOCIATION
201 Pryor Street, S.W.
Atlanta, Georgia 30303
(404) 688-0472

ASSOCIATION OF IDAHO CITIES
3100 South Vista Ave, Suite 310
Boise, Idaho 83705
(208) 344-8594

ILLINOIS MUNICIPAL LEAGUE
P.O. Box 5180 (500 E. Capitol Avenue - 62701)
Springfield, Illinois 62705-5180
(217) 525-1220

INDIANA ASSOCIATION OF CITIES AND TOWNS
200 S. Meridian Street, Suite 340
Indianapolis, Indiana 46225
(317) 237-6200

IOWA LEAGUE OF CITIES
317 Sixth Avenue, Suite 800
Des Moines, Iowa 50309-4111
(515) 244-7282

LEAGUE OF KANSAS MUNICIPALITIES
300 S.W. 8th Street
Topeka, Kansas 66603-3912
(785) 354-9565

KENTUCKY LEAGUE OF CITIES, INC.
100 East Vine Street, Suite 800
Lexington, Kentucky 40507-3700
(859) 977-3700

LOUISIANA MUNICIPAL ASSOCIATION
P.O. Box 4327 (700 North 10th Street - 70802)
Baton Rouge, Louisiana 70821
(225) 344-5001

MAINE MUNICIPAL ASSOCIATION
60 Community Drive
Augusta, Maine 04330
(207) 623-8428

MARYLAND MUNICIPAL LEAGUE
1212 West Street
Annapolis, Maryland 21401
(410) 268-5514

MASSACHUSETTS MUNICIPAL ASSOCIATION
One Winthrop Square
Boston, Massachusetts 02110
(617) 426-7272

MICHIGAN MUNICIPAL LEAGUE
P.O. Box 1487 (1675 Green Road - 48105-2530)
Ann Arbor, Michigan 48106-1487
(734) 662-3246

LEAGUE OF MINNESOTA CITIES
145 University Avenue, West
St. Paul, Minnesota 55103-2044
(651) 281-1200

MISSISSIPPI MUNICIPAL LEAGUE
600 East Amite Street, Suite 104
Jackson, Mississippi 39201
(601) 353-5854

MISSOURI MUNICIPAL LEAGUE
1727 Southridge Drive
Jefferson City, Missouri 65109
(573) 635-9134

MONTANA LEAGUE OF CITIES AND TOWNS
P.O. Box 1704
(208 North Montana - Suite 201- 59601)
Helena, Montana 59624-1704
(406) 442-8768

LEAGUE OF NEBRASKA MUNICIPALITIES
1335 L Street
Lincoln, Nebraska 68508
(402) 476-2829

NEVADA LEAGUE OF CITIES AND MUNICIPALITIES
310 South Curry Street
Carson City, Nevada 89703
(775) 882-2121

NEW HAMPSHIRE LOCAL GOVERNMENT CENTER
P.O. Box 617
(25 Triangle Park Drive - 03301)
Concord, New Hampshire 03302-0617
(603) 224-7447

NEW JERSEY STATE LEAGUE OF MUNICIPALITIES
222 West State Street
Trenton, New Jersey 08608
(609) 695-3481

NEW MEXICO MUNICIPAL LEAGUE
P.O. Box 846 (1229 Paseo de Peralta - 87501)
Santa Fe, New Mexico 87504-0846
(505) 982-5573

NEW YORK STATE CONFERENCE OF MAYORS & MUNICIPAL FFICIALS
119 Washington Avenue
Albany, New York 12210
(518) 463-1185

NORTH CAROLINA LEAGUE OF MUNICIPALITIES
P.O. Box 3069 (215 N. Dawson - 27602)
Raleigh, North Carolina, 27602-3609
(919) 715-4000

NORTH DAKOTA LEAGUE OF CITIES
410 E. Front Ave.

Bismarck, North Dakota 58504-5641
(701) 223-3518

OHIO MUNICIPAL LEAGUE
175 South Third Street, Suite 510
Columbus, Ohio 43215
(614) 221-4349

OKLAHOMA MUNICIPAL LEAGUE
201 North East 23rd Street
Oklahoma City, Oklahoma 73105
(405) 528-7515

LEAGUE OF OREGON CITIES
P.O. Box 928 (1201 Court Street, N.E., Suite 200 - 97301)
Salem, Oregon 97308
(503) 588-6550

PENNSYLVANIA LEAGUE OF CITIES AND MUNICIPALITIES
414 North Second Street
Harrisburg, Pennsylvania 17101
(717) 236-9469
1 State Street, Suite 502
Providence, Rhode Island 02908
(401) 272-3434

MUNICIPAL ASSOCIATION OF SOUTH CAROLINA
P.O. Box 12109
(1411 Gervais Street - 29201)
Columbia, South Carolina 29211
(803) 799-9574
214 East Capitol
Pierre, South Dakota 57501
(605) 224-8654

TENNESSEE MUNICIPAL LEAGUE
226 Capitol Blvd., Room 710
Nashville, Tennessee 37219-1894
(615) 255-6416

TEXAS MUNICIPAL LEAGUE
1821 Rutherford Lane, Suite 400
Austin, Texas 78754-5128
(512) 231-7400

UTAH LEAGUE OF CITIES & TOWNS
50 South 600 East, Suite 150
Salt Lake City, Utah 84102
(801) 328-1601

VERMONT LEAGUE OF CITIES AND TOWNS
89 Main Street, Suite 4
Montpelier, Vermont 05602-2948
(802) 229-9111

VIRGINIA MUNICIPAL LEAGUE
P.O. Box 12164
(13 East Franklin Street - 23219)
Richmond, Virginia 23241
(804) 649-8471

ASSOCIATION OF WASHINGTON CITIES
1076 South Franklin Street, SE
Olympia, Washington 98501-1346
(360) 753-4137

WEST VIRGINIA MUNICIPAL LEAGUE 2020 Kanawha Blvd. East
Charleston, West Virginia 25311
(304) 342-5564

LEAGUE OF WISCONSIN MUNICIPALITIES
202 State Street - Suite 300
Madison, Wisconsin 53703-2215
(608) 267-2380

WYOMING ASSOCIATION OF MUNICIPALITIES
315 West 27th Street
Cheyenne, Wyoming 82001
(307) 632-0398http://www.nlc.org/default.htm

Website Resource Guide For Youth and Community Related Grants

Below you will find WEB Addresses to organizations and agencies that offer grants to support worthy youth efforts. Some may offer "start-up" funds, which are funds that will help you along during the design phase of your program. There are also traditional grants that are available to your program. These traditional grants have certain criteria that must be met in order for your program to apply and receive grant funds. Please do not limit yourself to the list that I have provided, but explore the Internet for grant sources that meet your program's need. Keep in mind that there are government grants that may provide assistance to your program as well.

1. http://www.aecf.org/

2. http://www.afpnet.org/national_philanthropy_day_and_afp_awards/afps_awards_program

3. http://www.allstate.com/foundation/funding-guidelines.aspx

4. http://www.ameriprise.com/about-ameriprise-financial/company-information/ameriprise- community-relations.asp

5. http://www.annenbergfoundation.org/

6. http://www.arrlf.org/special_programs/VCC_youth_fund

7. http://www.aushermanfamilyfoundation.org/GrantApplications/

8. http://www.barronprize.org/

9. http://www.botball.org/funding-scholarships/cocacola_foundation_grant.php

10. http://www.broadfoundation.org/

11. http://www.brownfoundation.org/

12. http://www.buffettscholarships.org/

13. http://www.cct.org/

14. http://www.calendow.org/

15. http://www.calfund.org/

16. http://www.carnegie.org/

17. http://www.casey.org/

18. http://www.clevelandfoundation.org/

19. http://www.csrees.usda.gov/funding/rfas/rural_youthdev.html

20. http://www.ddcf.org/

21. http://www.danielsfund.org/

22. http://www.dosomething.org/grants/general/apply

23. http://www.dreyersinc.com/dreyersfoundation/large_grants.asp

24. http://www.dukeendowment.org/

25. http://edocket.access.gpo.gov/2009/pdf/E9-6320.pdf

26. http://edocket.access.gpo.gov/2009/pdf/E9-17921.pdf

27. http://www.energizeyourcommunity.com/Power_In_Numbers-DoSomething_Contest_Rules.pdf.

28. http://www.entergy.com/our_community/Grant_Guidelines.aspx

29. http://foundationcenter.org

30. http://foundationcenter.org/pnd/rfp/rfp_item.jhtml?id=99300038

31. http://www.fordfound.org/

32. http://www.gatesfoundation.org/Pages/home.aspx

33. http://www.getty.edu/

34. https://www.grantsolutions.gov/gs/preaward/previewPublicAnnouncement.do?id=10539

35. http://www.hearstfdn.org/

36. http://www.heinz.org/

37. http://www.hewlett.org/

38. http://www.hfg.org/

39. http://www.hjweinbergfoundation.org/

40. http://www.houstonendowment.org/

41. http://www.irvine.org/

42. http://www.jimjosephfoundation.org/

43. http://www.joycefdn.org/

44. www.jpmorganchase.com/cm/cs?pagename=Chase/Href&urlname=jpmc/community/grants

45. http://www.kauffman.org/

46. http://www.kidsconsortium.org/minigrants.php

47. http://www.kidsgardening.com/grants/naturalandnative.asp

48. http://www.kidsgardening.com/YGG.asp

49. http://www.kidsinneed.net/grants/

50. http://www.kindermorgan.com/community/

51. http://www.knightfoundation.org/

52. http://www.kresge.org/index.php/what/community_relief_fund/

53. http://www.legochildrensfund.org/Guidelines.html

54. http://www.lillyendowment.org/

55. http://www.lisc.org/section/goals/healthy/youth/request/

56. http://www.luminafoundation.org/

57. http://www.magicjohnson.com/index.php?/foundation/programs/community/

58. http://marybyronproject.org/CelebratingSolutions.html

59. http://www.mcknight.org/

60. http://www.mellon.org/

61. http://www.mfi.org/

62. http://mlb.mlb.com/mlb/official_info/community/btf.jsp?content=grant_process

63. http://www.moodyf.org/

64. http://www.moore.org/

65. http://www.msdf.org/

66. http://www.mott.org/

67. http://www.ncbrightideas.com/

68. http://www.nea.org/grants/awards/16212.htm

69. http://www.noble.org/

70. http://www.northropgrumman.com/corporate-responsibility/corporate-citizenship/foundation-grant-guidelines.html

71. http://www.nycommunitytrust.org/

72. http://www.packard.org/home.aspx

73. http://www.plt.org/cms/pages/21_22_21.html

74. http://www.rbf.org/?doc_id=801419

75. http://responsiblesports.com/community_grants/community_grant_details.aspx#
     Participate

76. http://rmhc.org/what-we-do/grants/

77. http://www.rockfound.org/

78. http://www.rwjf.org/

79. http://www.rwjf.org/applications/solicited/cfp.jsp?ID=20781

80. http://www.rwjf.org/applications/solicited/cfp.jsp?ID=20902

81. http://www.siliconvalleycf.org/

82. http://www.sloan.org/

83. http://www.statefarmyab.com/apply.php

84. http://www.starrfoundation.org/

85. http://www.sua.umn.edu/groups/funding/grants/apply/

86. http://www.tdbanknorth.com/community/housing_grant_competition.html

87. http://www.templeton.org/

88. http://www.techlearning.com/section/LeaderoftheYear

89. http://www.tomsofmaine.com/community-involvement/fifty-states.aspx

90. http://www.tolerance.org/teens/grants.jsp

91. http://www.tonyhawkfoundation.org/grant_application.asp

92. http://www.toolboxforeducation.com/

93. http://www.tulsacf.org/

94. http://www.uscc.com/uscellular/SilverStream/Pages/x_page.html?p=a_charitable_zips

95. http://www.vfw.org/index.cfm?fa=cmty.leveld&did=151

96. http://www.wallacefoundation.org/Pages/default.aspx

97. http://www.waltonfamilyfoundation.org/

98. http://www.williampennfoundation.org/

99. http://www.wkkf.org/Default.aspx?LanguageID=0

100. http://www.wmkeck.org/

101. http://www.woodruff.org/

Notes

Notes

Notes

Notes

Notes

Notes

Notes